PRAISE FOR *ASSURANCE OF ADOPTION*

"Nothing is more ultimate and more at stake in the salvation of Christians and for their assurance of salvation than their adoption by God as their Father in union with Christ (Rom 8:29). *Assurance of Adoption* explores this central truth in fresh, perceptive, and helpful ways. I commend its careful reading and study."

—RICHARD B. GAFFIN JR., Professor of Biblical and Systematic Theology, Emeritus, Westminster Theological Seminary

"Chun Tse presents us with a highly creative and thought-provoking approach to assurance, informed by careful study of the Holy Scriptures and reflection on the Reformed tradition. One need not agree with all his proposals in order to be enriched by his scholarly and fertile thinking. By centering assurance upon adoption in Christ, Tse offers biblical and holistic insights that, by God's grace, will not only enlighten the mind but also strengthen the soul."

—JOEL R. BEEKE, President, Puritan Reformed Theological Seminary, Grand Rapids, Michigan

"In drawing attention to the importance of adoption in the discussion of the assurance of salvation, Chun Tse's study provides a way to understand the relationship between the existential, judicial, relational, moral, and eschatological aspects of God's redemptive work through Christ. In doing so, an abstract doctrinal affirmation becomes directly relevant to the struggles of individual believers. Moving from historical and theological considerations to a careful examination of the biblical witnesses, readers are compelled to end in doxological exclamation in view of the incredible work of God that centers on Christ, the only foundation for a certainty that defies human weaknesses."

—DAVID W. PAO, Professor of New Testament and Chair of the New Testament Department, Trinity Evangelical Divinity School

"Written with the precision of an engineer and the heart of a pastor (Chun Tse is both), *Assurance of Adoption* comes as a welcome contribution to the growing corpus on the theology of adoption. Tse here restores Puritan advocacy for adoption's pastoral poignancy. But this is no mere recapitulation. Tse nimbly excavates adoption's storehouse of treasure for gospel assurance and distinctively unearths how and why 'Abba! Father' surges from the soul of the child of God."

—DAVID B. GARNER, Academic Dean and Vice President of Global Ministries, Associate Professor of Systematic Theology, Westminster Theological Seminary

"Real assurance of just about anything is in short order today. There are lots of promises in the advertising world that if you'll just call this number, or ask your doctor, you may aspire to a degree of certainty in a product. Chun Tse's study makes no such tentative conjectures. This is one of the most sure-footed guides to the question of assurance of salvation available. It takes us through the history of the subject, the wisdom of the confessions, but, most of all, the exegesis of Scripture, to ground assurance in its only sure source: the character of God. I highly recommend it to anyone wanting to know for sure if God loves them."

—WILLIAM EDGAR, Professor of Apologetics, Westminster Theological Seminary

"Chun Tse eloquently and persuasively shows that Christian assurance is grounded in our blood-bought adoption as children of God. Replete with skillful handling of biblical texts, *Assurance of Adoption* is cogently argued, historically informed, pastorally encouraging, compelling, and logical. Anyone seeking assurance of salvation in Christ in the Reformed tradition will find ample help in these pages."

—DANIEL M. GURTNER, former Ernest and Mildred Hogan Professor of New Testament Interpretation, Southern Baptist Theological Seminary

"Chun Tse has written a compelling and insightful book which challenges the contemporary church's neglect of the theology of adoption. Drawing on the wealth of the Reformed and Puritan traditions this work offers an important and timely perspective on assurance grounded in the Bible, centered on union with Christ, and intended for the enriching of faith and the consolation of the Christian soul."

—SIMON J. G. BURTON, John Laing Senior Lecturer in Reformation History, School of Divinity, University of Edinburgh

Assurance of Adoption

Assurance of Adoption

A New Paradigm for Assurance of Salvation

CHUN TSE

WIPF & STOCK · Eugene, Oregon

ASSURANCE OF ADOPTION
A New Paradigm for Assurance of Salvation

Wipf & Stock
An Imprint of Wipf and Stock Publishers
199 W. 8th Ave., Suite 3
Eugene, OR 97401

www.wipfandstock.com

PAPERBACK ISBN: 978-1-7252-8012-0
HARDCOVER ISBN: 978-1-7252-8013-7
EBOOK ISBN: 978-1-7252-8014-4

Manufactured in the U.S.A.   09/14/20

Dedicated to Vivian, Charis, Shulamite, and Eden

For all who are led by the Spirit of God are sons of God. For you did not receive the spirit of slavery to fall back into fear, but you have received the Spirit of adoption as sons, by whom we cry, "Abba! Father!" The Spirit himself bears witness with our spirit that we are children of God, and if children, then heirs—heirs of God and fellow heirs with Christ, provided we suffer with him in order that we may also be glorified with him.

ROMANS 8:14–17

Contents

PART V | PASTORAL IMPLICATIONS AND CONCLUSION

List of Tables

Preface

THIS BOOK PROPOSES A new paradigm for understanding assurance of salvation. My interest in assurance grows out of my own experience. When I received Christ in my sophomore year at college, my life was decisively transformed overnight. A supernatural love and joy took hold of me in such a compelling way that I could instantly forgive others in a way that I could not before. This excitement about the gospel was hard to contain—I began to share it with my professors and classmates, even strangers on the street. I absorbed the Bible and other spiritual books like a sponge. There was no doubt in my mind I was a child of God.

That level of assurance, however, proved to be short-lived. Following a few years of exponential growth in spiritual knowledge and practical living came the dreaded plateau, which lasted just as long. My hunger for all things spiritual subsided. The unceasing battles between the flesh and the Spirit were exhausting. My mind was baffled by many theological questions: How do I know I am a child of God? What if I am not one of God's elect? What if my faith is not real? My doubt was not about the efficacy of Christ's saving work, but whether I had truly believed. This uncertainty on the state of my soul was palpable—I even refrained from taking the elements of the Lord's Supper for a while, lest I would eat and drink judgment on myself. In short, I had lost the assurance of salvation, living in doubt instead of joy.

I shared this struggle with a Christian friend at church. She, being brought up in a Christian home, suggested that I start serving at church, which I did. Within merely two weeks of serving at a college fellowship, the assurance of salvation returned! A supernatural joy and heartfelt love from above once again filled me. Assurance, I realized then, is more than just knowledge of some biblical promises or a strong feeling. It also entails an exercise of one's will. By God's providence, this Christian who gave me this counsel eventually became my wife, and to her and our three daughters this book is dedicated.

My fascination with the topic of assurance continued to grow over the years. After becoming a pastor, assurance, I realized, is a shared concern not only for Christians but also for some seekers as well. It is a popular topic in every baptism class. It is preached from the pulpit and discussed in Sunday school. My interest in assurance drove me to an academic study of it, first at Bethel Seminary in Minnesota, then at Westminster Theological Seminary in Pennsylvania, and now at the University of Edinburgh in Scotland.

What exactly is assurance of salvation? What is the best interpretive angle to look at assurance? How is assurance understood by noted theologians and the Reformed confessions and catechisms? How is it described by the apostle Paul and the apostle John? How is assurance related to union with Christ, the *ordo salutis*, the sacraments, and Pentecost? This book addresses these questions by setting forth a new paradigm—assurance of adoption *is* assurance of salvation. The tenor of the book is that an adoption-centric understanding of assurance, based on union with Christ, most comprehensively captures the theological richness of salvation.

Authoring a book is never an individual effort. I especially appreciate my wife, Vivian, and our three daughters, Charis, Shulamite, and Eden, for their loving support, patience, and encouragement throughout the process of writing this book. Charis, in particular, has proofread a significant portion of this work and offered insightful comments, which is a delight to read as a father. Together they have taught me what it means to live as a family. I would like to thank my sister, Chloe Sun, who first introduced the gospel to my family. Thankfulness is also due, of course, to my parents, for their unceasing love.

I want to thank Dr. Lane Tipton for encouraging me to explore the adoption-centric understanding of assurance outlined in this book. I thank Dr. William Edgar for reading my work and encouraging me with his comments. I also greatly appreciate the encouragement of Drs. Daniel Gurtner, Aaron Denlinger, David Garner, Richard Gaffin Jr., Simon Burton, David Fergusson, Joel Beeke, David Pao, Sinclair Ferguson, and Kevin DeYoung.

I would like to thank all the staff at Wipf and Stock for a delightful experience in the process of publishing this book.

Thanks are also due to Pastor Paul Chang and Elder Daniel Luan for encouraging me in my theological pursuit. I am also grateful to God for the provision of a theological fund that made this study possible. My friend Heng Li Chiong has also provided me with useful theological resources, for which I am thankful. I would also like to acknowledge Sarah Lin for proofreading an earlier version of this work. The timely help provided by Karl Dahlfred, my fellow student at Edinburgh, is also gladly noted.

I appreciate the love and prayers of the brothers and sisters at Monmouth Community Christian Church in New Jersey, whom I had the privilege of shepherding during my study at Westminster Theological Seminary. God has also graced me and my family with love and prayers from the saints at Rutgers Community Christian Church in New Jersey, Chinese Bible Church at College Park in Maryland, Twin City Chinese Christian Church and Minnesota Mandarin Christian Church in Minnesota, Atlantic Chinese Alliance Church in New Jersey, Oversea Chinese Mission Church in New York, Calvary Baptist Church of New Haven in Connecticut, and Chinese Evangelical Church in Edinburgh, Scotland.

Above all, I thank my heavenly Father who loves me with an everlasting love in Christ through the Spirit. He would desire all his children to experience this same assurance. I now invite you to journey with me in this quest for assurance of adoption.

CHUN TSE
School of Divinity, New College
University of Edinburgh
August 12, 2020

Abbreviations

BDAG   Danker, Frederick William, ed. *A Greek-English Lexicon of the New Testament and Other Early Christian Literature.* 3rd ed. Chicago: University of Chicago Press, 2000.

HC   Heidelberg Catechism

WCF   Westminster Confession of Faith

WLC   Westminster Larger Catechism

WSC   Westminster Shorter Catechism

PART I

Assurance of Adoption

Chapter 1

Introduction

ASSURANCE OF SALVATION IS a subject at least as old as Christianity itself. It is a topic pregnant with immense theological as well as pastoral and personal significance. How can believers be sure whether they are children of God? What, exactly, is assurance of salvation? How should one understand and interpret assurance? How is it related to justification, adoption, sanctification, perseverance, and glorification? This chapter sheds some light on these questions by analyzing assurance from a theological perspective.

A. WHAT IS THE ASSURANCE OF SALVATION?

A person's understanding of assurance of salvation is a function of that person's theological tradition. To those who do not believe in the perseverance of the saints, assurance, if it exists, is only restricted to present salvation. They cannot extrapolate that confidence into the future because, as far as they know, salvation can be revoked, perhaps due to some grave sins that might be committed later in their lives for which they may not repent. They may enlist passages like Heb 6:4–8 as their support. Even those who believe a person's salvation, both now and in the future, is eternally secured in Christ may still lack *personal* assurance, especially when they ponder the discrepancy between how they live and how they ought to live. They may cite a passage like Rom 7:14–25 to justify their doubt. Others believe it is altogether impossible to obtain assurance as it is privileged and classified information only God possesses. Their proof text is Deut 29:29.

A person's understanding of both redemption and salvation also shapes that person's understanding of assurance.[1] From a divine perspective, redemption, rooted in the *historia salutis*,[2] is purposed by the Father before creation, accomplished by Christ in his death and resurrection, applied by the Spirit to believers, and will be consummated by the Triune God at the end of the eschatological age.[3] From the perspective of the redeemed, salvation, with its manifold riches reflected in the *ordo salutis*,[4] is actualized within the overarching framework of union with Christ.[5] Believers can only participate in the redemptive benefits accomplished by Christ through union with him by Spirit-wrought faith alone. It follows that assurance, being one of the spiritual blessings of salvation, necessarily flows from union with Christ.

A more fundamental question remains, however, regarding the intrinsic meaning of assurance of salvation. What is assurance of salvation? The simplicity of the question masks its complexity. If one views salvation in light of election, then assurance is being sure one is among the elect.[6] If one regards salvation as chiefly justification, then assurance is tantamount to believing in one's sins having been forgiven.[7] If one considers salvation's main thrust as regeneration[8] or sanctification,[9] then assurance is being sure one has been born again and has evidenced the fruit of the Spirit. If one understands salvation as adoption, then assurance implies a certainty of

---

1. Redemption is not the same as salvation. Redemption is what the Triune God needs to accomplish in order to secure the salvation of the elect. Salvation is the undoing of the effects of sin in the elect. Salvation, with its elements laid out in the *ordo salutis*, has a past, present, and future aspect, whereas redemption is rooted in the historical work of Jesus in the *historia salutis*. Elect are only saved when the Spirit applies the redemption accomplished by Christ to them through faith. Believers take no part in redemption but are urged to work out their salvation with fear and trembling (Phil 2:12).

2. This is a Latin term for the history of salvation.

3. The notion that redemption is "planned, accomplished, applied, and consummated" is articulated by Peterson, *Adopted by God*, 8.

4. This is a Latin term for the order of salvation. For a history of the development of this term, see Fesko, *Beyond Calvin*, 76–102.

5. The theological concept of "union with Christ" will be discussed at length in chapter 7.

6. Eph 1:4; Rom 9:11; 2 Tim 1:9.

7. Rom 3:25–26; 4:5; 8:1; 1 Cor 1:30; 2 Cor 5:21.

8. John 3:3–8; Ezek 36:25–27; Eph 2:4–5; Col 2:13; Titus 3:4–7.

9. Gal 5:22–23; 1 Cor 6:11; 1 Pet 1:5–8.

one's status as a child of God.[10] If one links salvation to perseverance,[11] then assurance entails confidence that God will preserve the Christian who will, in turn, endure to the end.[12] If one views salvation from the vantage point of death and glorification, then assurance is trusting that one will go to heaven upon death and will receive glorification when Christ returns.[13] While each perspective above is valid and can find scriptural support, this study argues that an adoption-centric understanding of assurance best encompasses the manifold theological richness of salvation.

In addition to delineating salvation, the meaning of assurance itself calls for a more precise understanding. Is assurance merely an intellectual assent to some objective truth about salvation? Is it a feeling, trust, confidence, or knowledge that one will go to heaven? Is assurance personal or is there a communal aspect to it? There is, therefore, a definite warrant for a more biblically robust understanding of assurance, which is the subject of this book.

D. A. Carson defines assurance as a believer's confidence that "he or she is already in a right standing with God, and that this will issue in ultimate salvation."[14] There is a present as well as a future aspect of assurance in this definition. A more straightforward definition—assurance is confidence of final salvation—is proposed by Robert Peterson.[15] J. I. Packer defines assured faith in the New Testament as having a double object:

> First, God's revealed truth, viewed comprehensively as a promise of salvation in Christ; second, the believer's own interest in that promise. In both cases, the assurance is correlative to and derived from divine testimony.[16]

The emphasis here is not so much the present versus the future aspect of assurance but the objective versus the subjective basis of it. The objective ground of assurance is God's revealed truth, whereas the subjective basis is the believer's interest in that promise.

---

10. Rom 8:14–17; Eph 1:5; John 1:12; Gal 4:5.

11. John 10:28–29; Rom 8:31–39; 1 Cor 1:4–9; Heb 7:25; 1 Pet 1:3–5.

12. Multiple New Testament Scriptures testify to the eternal security of believers: John 3:15–16; 5:24; 6:37–39; 10:28–29; Rom 8:31–39; 11:29; 2 Cor 1:22; Eph 1:13–14; 2:8; 4:30; Phil 1:6; Heb 7:25; 13:5; 1 John 5:10–13; Jude 24.

13. 1 Cor 15:50–53; Rom 8:23, 30.

14. Carson, "Reflections on Christian Assurance," 1–2.

15. Peterson, *Our Secure Salvation*, 200.

16. Packer, "Assurance," 95–96.

This book defines assurance of salvation in light of adoption, which manifests and subordinates to union with Christ.[17] Since believers can only participate in the redemptive benefits of Christ through union with him by Spirit-wrought faith, it follows that assurance, as one of the spiritual blessings of salvation, stems from and is under the overarching framework of union with Christ.[18] Specifically, *assurance of salvation, as a redemptive benefit flowing from union with Christ, is the true confidence that a person is an adopted child of God now and forever.*

B. CONTEMPORARY WORKS OF ASSURANCE OF SALVATION

Contemporary works on assurance are multitudinous. The following is a sampling of writings on this perennial issue, written from the historical, exegetical, and theological perspectives.

Written from the perspective of historical theology, Joel Beeke examines the views of Reformers and Puritans on assurance. Specifically, he studies the apparent disparity between "Calvin and the Calvinists" concerning whether assurance is of the essence of faith.[19] Robert Letham, in his doctoral study, delves into the relationship between saving faith and assurance in the Swiss, Bucerian, and Genevan Impartation, and also in German Reformed, British, and Dutch Reformed theology, ending the study at the Synod of Dort.[20] Jonathan Master details the history of the development of this doctrine after the Westminster Confession.[21] Other scholars have written on the theology of assurance of noted theologians, such as M. Charles Bell on Calvin and Scottish theologians,[22] Randall Zachman on Luther and Calvin,[23]

---

17. As stated in Westminster Larger Catechism A. 69, adoption, like justification and sanctification, manifests believers' union with Christ.

18. Union with Christ is more primary than assurance. A person can say, "I have assurance because I am united to Christ," but it would not be correct to say, "I am united to Christ because I have assurance."

19. Beeke, *Assurance of Faith*; Beeke, "Faith and Assurance"; Beeke, "Personal Assurance of Faith"; Beeke, "Calvin and the Calvinists," 43–71; Beeke, *Quest for Full Assurance*; Beeke, *Knowing and Growing*.

20. Letham, "Saving Faith and Assurance in Reformed Theology."

21. Master, *Question of Consensus*.

22. Bell, *Calvin and Scottish Theology*.

23. Zachman, *Assurance of Faith*.

Eric Rivera on William Gouge,[24] Mark Noll on John Wesley,[25] Richard Snoddy on James Ussher,[26] and Keith Stanglin on Jacobus Arminius.[27]

Written from the vantage point of exegetical and biblical theology, Martyn Lloyd-Jones studies the high priestly prayer of Jesus in John 17 in which assurance is a dominant theme.[28] Christopher Bass argues from the First Epistle of John that assurance is grounded in the atoning work of Christ but supported by the lifestyle of believers.[29] D. A. Carson has surveyed the broader corpus of the apostle John's writings on this topic.[30] Robert Gundry[31] and Judith Volf[32] have written on the theology of assurance of the apostle Paul. Thomas Schreiner and Ardel Caneday deal with the warning passages in the New Testament on perseverance and assurance.[33] Matthew Hoskinson[34] and Michael Eaton[35] attempt to construct a New Testament theology of hope and assurance.

Written from the angle of systematic theology, Louis Berkhof's classic little book *The Assurance of Faith*, written in 1938, explores the connection between faith and assurance, and the foundation and cultivation of assurance.[36] Herman Bavinck, in *The Certainty of Faith*, presents a philosophical, presuppositional, and theological defense of assurance in the Reformed tradition after considering the positions of non-Christians, Roman Catholics, Eastern Orthodox, and Protestants.[37]

Other than the more scholarly publications above, works targeting a more popular audience are too numerous to catalog. Among the more recent ones include such works by Greg Gilbert,[38] Robert Peterson,[39] and

24. Rivera, *Christ Is Yours*.
25. Noll, "John Wesley and Assurance."
26. Snoddy, *Soteriology of James Ussher*, 177–232.
27. Stanglin, *Arminius on Assurance*.
28. Lloyd-Jones, *Assurance of Our Salvation*.
29. Bass, *That You May Know*.
30. Carson, "Johannine Perspectives on Assurance."
31. Gundry, "Grace, Works, and Staying Saved."
32. Volf, *Paul and Perseverance*.
33. Schreiner and Caneday, *Race Set Before Us*.
34. Hoskinson, *Assurance of Salvation*.
35. Eaton, *No Condemnation*.
36. Berkhof, *Assurance of Faith*.
37. Bavinck, *Certainty of Faith*.
38. Gilbert, *Assured*.
39. Peterson, *Assurance of Salvation*.

Donald Whitney.[40] The constant stream of literature on assurance, at both the scholarly and popular level, bespeaks the ever-present interest in and significance of this topic.

C. CONTRIBUTION OF THE BOOK

The main contribution of this book is threefold. First, I will present an adoption-centric understanding of assurance. The argument is that adoption, more than any other element in the *ordo salutis*, provides a more comprehensive and theologically rich motif in understanding assurance. Most succinctly, assurance of adoption *is* assurance of salvation. Past scholarship has not sufficiently accentuated this adoption-centric perspective on assurance.

Second, assurance will be centered *explicitly* on the theological notion of union with Christ. The historical work of assurance, either during the Reformation or beyond, has not positioned assurance *explicitly* in the theological framework of union with Christ.[41] For instance, assurance, as stated in the Westminster Shorter Catechism A. 36, is a benefit flowing from "justification, adoption, and sanctification," which in turn, in Reformed theology, flows from union with Christ. Assurance, in this sense, is a *derived* benefit of union with Christ rather than a *direct* benefit. The connection between assurance and union with Christ is, in other words, implicit, not explicit. However, this study argues that assurance, being one of the benefits of salvation, flows directly and explicitly from union with Christ.

Third, since past scholarship has not listed assurance as an element of the *ordo salutis*, I will, as an exercise in constructive theology, incorporate assurance into a novel, modified *ordo salutis*, taking into account the existential, judicial, relational, moral, and eschatological dimensions of both salvation and assurance.

D. ORGANIZATION OF THE BOOK

The scope of this book is limited to studying the assurance of new covenant believers instead of old covenant saints. As such, the thesis statement I seek to defend is: *An adoption-centric understanding of assurance, which itself is*

---

40. Whitney, *How Can I Be Sure?*

41. Some may argue that a few Puritans, like Richard Sibbes, employ the concept of "comfort" as a close synonym for assurance, and the marriage metaphor in the Song of Songs as a proxy for union with Christ. See Sibbes, *Works of Richard Sibbes*, 22–31, 171–81.

a redemptive benefit of union with Christ, most comprehensively captures the theological richness of salvation.

This statement has two main parts. It encapsulates, first, an adoptive view of assurance. Second, it situates assurance of salvation within the framework of union with Christ, which is the fountainhead of all the redemptive benefits.

This book organizes into five parts with two chapters each. Part I, "Assurance of Adoption," discusses the complexities of understanding assurance of salvation. After orienting the readers to a theological analysis of assurance in the present chapter, we will delineate the linchpin of the book, an adoption-centric understanding of assurance of salvation, in chapter 2. It examines how assurance connects with other redemptive benefits such as regeneration, justification, adoption, sanctification, and glorification. Specifically, it contrasts the Pauline emphasis on adoption with the Johannine stress on the new birth. It then traces the fivefold usage of the exclusively Pauline term υἱοθεσία (adoption) and discusses the multidimensional nature of assurance.

Part II, "Historical Analysis," examines assurance from the perspective of historical theology and church history. Chapter 3 presents the views of Thomas Aquinas, Martin Luther, John Calvin, William Perkins, and John Wesley. Since an adoption-centric understanding of assurance is a new paradigm and construct, the purpose of this chapter is not so much to defend it but to provide a historical orientation to the topic. Chapter 4 studies how the Reformed confessions and catechisms in the sixteenth and seventeenth centuries approach assurance. The emphasis is on comparing the formulations of Heidelberg Catechism and Westminster Confession of Faith on assurance, especially on their view of whether assurance is of the essence of faith.

Part III, "Exegetical Analysis," scrutinizes assurance based on exegetical and biblical theology. Chapter 5 is an exegetical-theological study of Rom 8:12–17, which is the central scriptural locus for an adoption-centric understanding of assurance. A detailed exegesis of this critical passage demonstrates that assurance of adoption is assurance of salvation. Chapter 6 delves into a New Testament book written with the express purpose of giving its readers assurance of salvation. That book, of course, is 1 John. The three well-known cardinal tests of assurance—the tests of belief, righteousness, and love—will be scrutinized, beyond which I will discuss an additional test—the internal witness of the Spirit. The chapter also compares the view of assurance of the apostle John with that of the apostle Paul.

Part IV, "Theological Analysis," studies assurance from the perspective of systematic theology. Chapter 7 establishes the thesis that assurance is a redemptive benefit flowing from union with Christ, which is the organizing principle of redemptive benefits. It examines how believers' union with the resurrected Christ has borne on the doctrine of assurance. Chapter 8 explores how assurance is related to the *ordo salutis*, the sacraments, and the Pentecost. In particular, I will incorporate assurance into a novel, modified *ordo salutis*, taking into account the existential, judicial, relational, moral, and eschatological dimensions of both assurance and salvation.

Finally, in Part V, "Pastoral Implications and Conclusion," I will discuss some applications of the adoption-centric view of assurance in chapter 9 and conclude this study in chapter 10.

At the end of each chapter, starting with chapter 2, comments will be made concerning the well-known historical question, "Is assurance of the essence of faith?" All Scriptures cited are from the English Standard Version (ESV) unless stated otherwise.

E. SUMMARY

A person's understanding of assurance is a direct function of the corresponding understanding of salvation, which is based on the redemptive work of the Triune God and distinguished from it. Assurance is a redemptive benefit of union with Christ, which entails real confidence that a person is an adopted child of God now and forever. The next chapter will further scrutinize the inherent connection between adoption and assurance.

Chapter 2

Assurance of Adoption Is
Assurance of Salvation

Since one can view salvation from different angles, is there a specific angle from which one can see salvation in its brightest light and fullest splendor? Is assurance based solely on the objective promises of God, or is there a subjective ground for it? Is assurance a part of faith, or is it distinct from it? What is the significance of the threefold basis of assurance? This chapter explores these questions and introduces the concept of an adoption-centric understanding of salvation. It establishes the thesis that assurance of adoption is assurance of salvation.

A. A SYSTEMATIC-THEOLOGICAL VIEW OF ASSURANCE OF SALVATION

The anatomy of assurance of salvation starts with the anatomy of salvation, which can be regarded as the acts and the works of the Triune God to undo the damaging effects of the original sin. Due to the disobedience of Adam (Gen 3:6), the federal representative head of humanity, all human beings have sinned in his sin. As a result, five detrimental consequences befall his posterity.

Existentially, because of Adam's sin, humanity is dead, spiritually, in the death of Adam (Gen 2:17; Rom 5:12, 17; Eph 2:1). Regeneration is the

Spirit's act to revive this death in which the elect receive a new spiritual life (John 3:5; Eph 2:5; 1 Cor 15:22).

Judicially, all humanity is guilty in the guilt of Adam (Rom 5:12–21). Justification is God's forensic act of removing this guilt in which the elect first impute their sins to Christ, who bore those sins on their behalf (Isa 53:5; 2 Cor 5:21; 1 Pet 2:24; 3:18) and died for them vicariously (Rom 4:25, 5:8). Then, by grace through faith alone in Jesus and his atonement work on the cross, Christ's righteousness is imputed to those who believe (Eph 2:8; Rom 3:24–26, 10:9; Acts 16:31).

Relationally, humanity is alienated from God in the alienation of Adam (Col 1:21–22). The relationship between humanity and God has become estranged and antagonistic (Gen 3:8; John 3:19–20; 2 Cor 5:18; Eph 2:3). Adoption is God's act to restore this estrangement by receiving the elect into his family (Eph 1:5; Gal 4:5; Rom 8:15, 23; 9:4). God is now the Heavenly Father of the redeemed, who are now brothers and sisters in God's family.

Morally, humanity is corrupted in the corruption of Adam, resulting in the total depravity of sinners. Sanctification is the Spirit's transformative work to renovate this corruption.[1] The Holy Spirit definitively, positionally, progressively, eschatologically, and finally sanctifies the elect.

Finally, sin has marred the *imago Dei* (God's image) in humans. Humanity, consequently, bears the shame and suffering of Adam.[2] Glorification is God's work of transforming this predicament. God replaces believers' shame with glory through progressive glorification in this life (2 Cor 3:18). In the life to come, God will also end all sufferings of believers upon their death (Rev 21:4) in eschatological glorification. In the final glorification, believers will receive their resurrected bodies at Christ's return (Rom 8:17). Table 1 summarizes the curses of sin and God's remedies in salvation.

---

1. Both regeneration and sanctification create internal moral transformation in the lives of believers by the Spirit. The two are so intimately related that John Calvin, in his *Institutes*, often uses "regeneration" as a synonym for "sanctification." Cornelis Venema comments, "Though referring to the same subject and issue, Calvin ordinarily uses the terminology of 'justification' and 'regeneration' or 'repentance.' Only infrequently does he speak of 'sanctification,' though it is clearly for him a synonym for either regeneration or repentance." Venema, *Accepted and Renewed*, 9.

2. Adam and Eve, after their sin, immediately felt shame, covered themselves, and hid from God (Gen 3:7–10). God cursed the earth, and suffering ensued immediately, which is a reality of life (Gen 3:16–19; Job 5:7; John 16:33).

Table 1: The curses of sin and the blessings of salvation

Dimension	Union with Adam Brings	Union with Christ Brings	Blessings of Salvation
Existential	Death	New spiritual life	Regeneration
Judicial	Guilt	Forgiveness of sins, righteousness	Justification
Relational	Estrangement	Reconciliation to become sons of God	Adoption
Moral	Corruption	Holiness	Sanctification
Eschatological[3]	Shame and Suffering	Glory	Glorification

In short, the death, guilt, estrangement, corruption, shame, and suffering brought by sin are rectified, respectively, through regeneration, justification, adoption, sanctification, and glorification. All these are redemptive benefits flowing from union with Christ. It is when Christ, by his resurrection,[4] is justified,[5] adopted,[6] sanctified,[7] and glorified[8] that believers in union with him can receive resurrection (regeneration),[9] justification,[10] adoption,[11] sanctification,[12] and glorification.[13] As such, the justification, adoption, sanctification, and glorification of believers are not separate acts,

---

3. As shall be displayed throughout the book, there is a sense in which all redemptive benefits, not just glorification, is eschatological.

4. Christ's resurrection is a bodily resurrection (John 2:19–21; Luke 24:38–39).

5. Christ is justified in the sense that in his resurrection, the Spirit vindicated his righteousness (1 Tim 3:16). As Richard Gaffin argues, "The constitutive, transforming action of resurrection is specifically forensic. It is Christ's justification." Gaffin, *Centrality of the Resurrection*, 124.

6. Christ is adopted in the sense that in his resurrection, "he was declared to be the Son of God in power" (Rom 1:4). Robert Peterson identifies four historical declarations of Jesus' adoption: his baptism (Matt 3:17), transfiguration (Matt 17:1–13), resurrection (Acts 13:27–30), and ascension (Heb 1:3–5). Peterson, *Adopted by God*, 59–63. For a detailed argument for and exposition of Jesus' adoption, see Garner, *Sons in the Son*, 173–218.

7. Christ is sanctified in the sense that in his resurrection, he died to sin once and for all but lives to God (Rom 6:10) and became believers' sanctification (1 Cor 1:30).

8. Christ, at his resurrection, was declared the Son of God in power (Rom 1:4), received a glorified, spiritual body, and became a life-giving Spirit (1 Cor 15:45). Gaffin, "Redemption and Resurrection," 21–26.

9. Rom 6:4–5,11; Eph 2:5–6; Col 2:12, 3:1.

10. 1 Cor 1:30; 2 Cor 5:21; Gal 2:17; Rom 8:1.

11. Gal 4:4–6; Rom 8:14–17.

12. 1 Cor 1:30; 6:11; Rom 6:1–23.

13. Rom 8:17, 23; Col 3:4; Phil 3:20–21; 1 Thess 4:16–17.

as Richard Gaffin concludes, but are "different facets or aspects of the one act of incorporation with the resurrected Christ."[14]

Assurance of salvation, then, is the confidence a person is regenerated, justified, adopted, sanctified, and glorified, through union with Christ. This understanding of assurance, indeed, was reflected in the language of the Westminster divines when they penned the Westminster Confession of Faith. Section 2 of chapter 18, entitled "Of the Assurance of Grace and Salvation," states:

> This certainty is not a bare conjectural and probable persuasion grounded upon a fallible hope; but an infallible assurance of faith founded upon the divine truth of the promises of salvation, the inward evidence of those graces unto which these promises are made, the testimony of the Spirit of adoption witnessing with our spirits that we are the children of God, which Spirit is the earnest of our inheritance, whereby we are sealed to the day of redemption.

Here, the "divine truth of the promises of salvation" corresponds primarily to justification. The "inward evidence of those graces unto which these promises are made" points to the fruits of regeneration and sanctification, both internally in believers' hearts (mystical syllogism) and externally in their lives (practical syllogism).[15] The "testimony of the Spirit of adoption witnessing with our spirits that we are the children of God" speaks of the Spirit's ministry of confirming the adoption of believers. Finally, the clause "we are sealed to the day of redemption" implies perseverance and glorification. Among these various redemptive benefits stemming from union with Christ, adoption is the highest and most comprehensive benefit encompassing the existential, judicial, relational, moral, and eschatological dimensions of salvation.[16]

Adoption is existential because there was a time when believers, before adoption, were strangers and aliens to the family of God (Eph 2:19a). They were not only children of wrath by nature (Eph 2:3) but, indeed, spiritually

---

14. Gaffin, *Resurrection and Redemption*, 130–31.

15. Though the language of the confession—"inward graces"—points more toward the internal changes in the heart rather than the external behavioral changes.

16. The view of adoption presented in this book slightly differs from the theology of adoption found in the Westminster Standards. Specifically, adoption, as stated in Westminster Larger Catechism A. 74 and Westminster Shorter Catechism A. 34, is an *act* of the free grace of God, whereas, in this book, adoption is *both an act and a work* of God. Nevertheless, that is not a problem for the present monograph, since it aims to express an exegetically creative theology that advances beyond the view of adoption found in the Westminster Standards.

dead (Eph 2:1). Believers have become members of the household of God only through the grace of adoption (Eph 2:19b).

Adoption is judicial as it involves a change of status of the elect from being enemies of God to being sons of God. While justification is also judicial, it only changes the elect's forensic standing before God's law from guilty to innocent; it stops short of elevating their status from innocence to sonship. This latter translation to sonship is through the act of divine adoption, which presupposes justification but is a higher privilege than it, as James Buchanan writes:

> According to the Scriptures, pardon, acceptance, and adoption, are distinct privileges, the one rising above the other in the order in which they have been stated; . . . while the two first properly belong to his justification, as being both founded on the same relation—that of a Ruler and Subject—the third is radically distinct from them, as being founded on a nearer, more tender, and more endearing relation—that between a Father and his Son.[17]

Adoption is, of course, intrinsically relational. Those adopted into the family of God have a filial relationship with God as their Heavenly Father. They also have a brotherly relationship with other Christians in the family, with Jesus himself as their Elder Brother (Heb 2:11).

Adoption is also morally transformative as it is the means through which believers are made "holy and blameless" before God, the *telos* of divine election (Eph 1:4–5). God predestines believers "for adoption (υἱοθεσίαν) as sons through Jesus Christ" to transform them into the likeness of his Son. When God brings the elect into his family through adoption, they are living in an environment in which they can continue to grow in their sanctification. God does not merely adopt the elect into his family and become an absentee Father afterward. Within the intimate Father-son relationship, the adopted children are continuously being "pitied, protected, provided for, and chastened by Him as by a Father."[18] In this sense, while adoption itself is a decisive act of God by which the elect's judicial status has changed from being outside of God's family to being sons of God, the subsequent outworking of this adoptive relationship is transformative, with the express purpose of renovating and conforming believers to the moral likeness of God's Son, the Elder Brother in God's family (Rom 8:29).

Finally, adoption, like other redemptive benefits such as justification and sanctification, is also eschatological. Carrying on the insights from the

17. Buchanan, *Doctrine of Justification*, 276.

18. The language is taken from Westminster Confession of Faith chapter 12 on adoption.

works of Herman Ridderbos and Geerhardus Vos, Richard Gaffin persuasively argues that since believers have yet to receive their resurrected bodies,
it is in that sense that they still await their justification when, in the Day
of Judgment, they shall be "openly acknowledged and acquitted" as being
righteous.[19] Besides, at death, a Christian's soul passes into heaven and is
eschatologically, immediately, and wholly sanctified to attain to eschatological sanctification. This is when the person's progressive sanctification
finally achieves the reality promised in the positional sanctification. Likewise, believers are already adopted (Rom 8:15; Gal 4:5) but are awaiting
their final adoption, the redemption of their bodies (Rom 8:23). The reality
of the eschatological benefits of adoption, however, has already dawned in
the present age.

When one simplistically equates salvation with either justification,
sanctification, or glorification, assurance translates to ascertaining one's
legal status before God's law, examining for one's fruit of the Spirit, or specu-
lating about one's future estate before God. If one views salvation from the
perspective of adoption, which simultaneously manifests the existential, legal, relational, moral, and eschatological aspects of salvation, it will capture
most comprehensively the theological richness of salvation. Put otherwise,
an adoption-centric understanding of assurance provides a more theologically rich and comprehensive motif in understanding salvation itself. It thus
behooves believers to embrace an adoption-centric rather than a justification-centric or sanctification-centric understanding of assurance.

Indeed, adoption, from the perspective of believers as the beneficiaries
of redemption, is the highest and most comprehensive benefit of salvation.[20]
From a divine perspective, however, adoption is for Christ, the benefactor
of believers' adoption. The Westminster Confession of Faith chapter 12, on
adoption, plainly teaches:

> All those that are justified, God vouchsafeth, *in* and *for His only
> Son Jesus Christ*, to make partakers of the grace of adoption: by
> which they are taken into the number, and enjoy the liberties
> and privileges of the children of God; have His name put upon
> them, receive the Spirit of adoption; have access to the throne of
> grace with boldness; are enabled to cry, Abba, Father; are pitied,
> protected, provided for, and chastened by Him as by a Father;
> yet never cast off, but sealed to the day of redemption, and in-
> herit the promises, as heirs of everlasting salvation.

19. Gaffin, *By Faith, Not by Sight*, 93–94.

20. "Adoption," J. I. Packer famously says, "is the highest privilege that the gospel
offers: higher even than justification." Packer, *Knowing God*, 206.

Adoption, noted by the Westminster divines, is both *in* Christ, regarding its means, and *for* Christ, regarding its goal. When sinners are redeemed and adopted as sons of God, it is for the pleasure of Christ who, by his resurrection, became "the firstfruits of those who have fallen asleep" (1 Cor 15:20). Christ, in this way, sees the adopted sons as the fruits of his travail on the cross and is satisfied.

B. THE DOCTRINE OF ADOPTION

1. Historical Neglect of the Doctrine of Adoption

The historical neglect of the doctrine of adoption by theologians has been well-documented.[21] The Southern Presbyterian theologian Robert A. Webb (1856–1919) says:

> The evangelical doctrine of Adoption—succinctly described as "an act of God's free grace, whereby we are received into the number, and have a right to all the privileges, of the sons of God"—has received but slender treatment at the hands of theologians. It has been handled with a meagreness entirely out of proportion to its intrinsic importance, and with a subordination which allows it only a parenthetical place in the system of evangelical truth.[22]

Reformed Protestant theologians like Francis Turretin, Charles Hodge, Louis Berkhof, and Anthony Hoekema devote little attention to adoption compared to justification and sanctification.[23] A notable exception is John Calvin, sometimes called "*the* theologian of adoption,"[24] who devotes extensive attention to this topic in his *Institutes*.[25] Paradoxically, though Calvin dedicates eight chapters of his *Institutes* to expound on the doctrine of

21. Trumper, "History of Adoption I," 4–28; Peterson, *Adopted by God*, 6–7; Trumper, *When History Teaches Us Nothing*, 1–32; Beeke, *Heirs with Christ*, 1–3. For a summary of the development of the doctrine of adoption in historical theology, see Garner, *Sons in the Son*, 20–34.

22. Webb, *Reformed Doctrine of Adoption*, 17.

23. Peterson, *Adopted by God*, 6.

24. Trumper, "History of Adoption II," 182.

25. After Calvin, the two theologians who arguably made the most contribution to the doctrine of adoption are John L. Girardeau (1825–98) and Robert A. Webb (1856–1919). See Girardeau, *Discussions of Theological Questions*, 428–521; Webb, *Reformed Doctrine of Adoption*, 5–188. In addition, Douglas F. Kelly keenly observes that "the theme of adoption has been seriously developed only among Reformed Christians of Celtic background." Kelly, "Adoption," 110–20.

justification, there is no specific chapter on adoption.[26] One can understand this apparent incongruity by recognizing adoption, just like union with Christ, as a permeating concept that defies confinement to isolated chapters in Calvin's writings.[27] "Adoption," argues David Garner, "is not a chapter in the *Institutes* because adoption is not reducible to a sequestered chapter in dogmatics."[28]

Still, Calvin's famous expression *duplex gratia Dei* (twofold grace of God)—justification and sanctification—also leaves out adoption.[29] Adoption, then, appears to occupy a less prominent position in Calvin's thought compared with justification and sanctification. A closer examination of how Calvin first introduces this terminology, however, reveals something different. The concept of *duplex gratia* first appears in the *Institutes* in the following:

> Christ was given to us by God's generosity, to be grasped and possessed by us in faith. By partaking of him, we principally receive a double grace: namely, that being reconciled to God through Christ's blamelessness, we may have in heaven instead of a Judge a gracious Father; and secondly, that sanctified by Christ's spirit we may cultivate blamelessness and purity of life.[30]

Calvin describes the first grace primarily as a reconciliation—the restoration of a broken relationship, which is the language reminiscent of adoption. This adoptive language turns explicit when Calvin asserts that God, as a consequence of reconciliation, becomes "instead of a Judge, a gracious *Father*." Hence, though the first benefit depicts justification, it has elements of adoption because justification, in itself, does not render God the Judge as God the Father. Regarding the second grace of the *duplex gratia*, having attained "Christ's blamelessness" through justification, believers may cultivate this blamelessness and purity of life through the Spirit's sanctification. This cultivation unto holiness is a process in which the Spirit, in conjunction with the "gracious Father," grooms the believers to mature in Christ. One cannot help but conjure up the imagery of parenting—spiritual parenting, in this case—in which children are cultivated to

---

26. In particular, chapters 11–14 from book III have specific titles on justification, and chapters 15–18 have specific sections within the chapters on justification.

27. "The importance of a doctrine for Calvin," Trumper notes, "is determined not by the number of chapters allotted to its discussion but how pervasively it is referred to throughout his work." Trumper, "History of Adoption II," 183.

28. Garner, *Sons in the Son*, 24.

29. Venema, "Twofold Grace of God," 67–105.

30. Calvin, *Institutes*, 3.11.1 (725).

grow in maturity. This sanctification, in other words, happens in the context of adoption. Therefore, Calvin, in speaking of the *duplex gratia*, conceives not merely of justification and sanctification, but he embeds the concept of adoption as well. "The adoption of believers," Howard Griffith comments, "is at the heart of John Calvin's understanding of salvation."[31]

The New Testament speaks of two distinct, necessary, simultaneous, and complementary ways of joining the family of God—via regeneration and adoption. As J. I. Packer puts it, "Adoption and regeneration accompany each other as two aspects of the salvation that Christ brings (John 1:12–13), but they are to be distinguished. Adoption is the bestowal of a relationship, while regeneration is the transformation of our moral nature. However, the link is evident; God wants his children, whom he loves, to bear his character, and takes action accordingly."[32]

2. Joining God's Family through Regeneration

The apostle John, in his writings, often stresses being born into God's family by the Spirit.[33] He records Jesus' words to Nicodemus, "Unless one is born of water and the Spirit, he cannot enter the kingdom of God" (John 3:5).[34] The apostle John is the only New Testament writer who employs the unique phrase "born of God" (ἐκ τοῦ θεοῦ γεγέννηται, γεγεννημένος ἐκ τοῦ θεοῦ, γεγεννημένον ἐκ τοῦ θεοῦ) or "born of him" (ἐξ αὐτοῦ γεγέννηται) to refer to Christians.[35] His favorite expression for Christians is "children of God" (τέκνα θεοῦ, τέκνα τοῦ θεοῦ)[36] and his customary title for God is "Father."[37]

Clearly, at the center of John's thought is the motif that people are born into God's family. These people, now with the same Heavenly Father, become children of God and brothers and sisters of one another. John's thesis is that those who exhibit this love toward God, as expressed through their love toward one another, have been born of God and have eternal life (1 John 4:7).

31. Griffith, "'First Title of the Spirit,'"135. See also Westhead, "Adoption in John Calvin."

32. Packer, *Concise Theology*, 168.

33. John 3:3–8. Cf. Ezek 36:25–27; Eph 2:4–5; Col 2:13; Tit 3:4–7.

34. The Old Testament reference of being born by water and Spirit is found in Ezekiel 36, where the water there signifies spiritual cleansing from sins. "The conjunction of water and Spirit in eschatological hope is deeply rooted in the Jewish consciousness, as is attested by Ezek 36:25–27 and various apocalyptic writings," says Beasley-Murray, *John*, 49.

35. All six occurrences are in the First Epistle of John: 2:29; 3:9; 4:7; 5:1, 4, 18.

36. 1 John 3:1, 2, 10; 5:2.

37. 1 John 1:2, 3; 2:1, 13, 15–16, 22–24; 3:1; 4:14; 5:1.

The apostle John explicitly states the purpose of his first epistle in 5:13, "I write these things to you who believe in (πιστεύητε εἰς) the name of the Son of God that you may know that you have eternal life (ζωὴν αἰώνιον)." First John was written, in other words, to assure true believers of their salvation. This understanding of assurance, however, is about having "eternal life," the life born of water and the Spirit (John 3:5). The apostle John thus holds to a regeneration-centric understanding of assurance based on viewing salvation as the new birth.

3. Joining God's Family through Adoption

The apostle Paul writes of entering God's family by adoption, which presupposes regeneration but goes much further. The term υἱοθεσία (adoption) is used exclusively by the apostle Paul, appearing five times in Romans, Galatians, and Ephesians altogether, arguably three of his most doctrine-intensive epistles. The semantic range of υἱοθεσία, concludes James Scott, has a Hellenistic meaning of "setting someone as a son" or "putting someone in the place of a son." The word υἱοθεσία is a compound word of two parts: υἱός, which means "son," and θεσία, derived from τίθημι, which means "to set, put, place."[38]

Paul's motif of adoption, most scholars agree, comes from the Greco-Roman social context, since the Jews did not practice the legal act of adoption. An adoptive parent could confer on the adopted child all the legal rights of a natural child, including receiving an inheritance. Significantly, in contrast to modern-day adoption in the Western world, adoption in the Greco-Roman world was chiefly for the adoptive parent to carry on the family name and pass on the family wealth, rather than for the benefits of the adopted sons.[39]

C. AN ADOPTION-CENTRIC UNDERSTANDING OF ASSURANCE OF SALVATION

From a redemptive-historical perspective, we can trace this fivefold usage of υἱοθεσία as follows, namely, the *authoring* of adoption (Eph 1:5), the *anticipation* of adoption (Rom 9:4), the *arrival* of adoption (Gal 4:4–5), the *assurance* of adoption (Rom 8:15), and the *achievement* of adoption (Rom 8:23).[40]

38. Scott, *Adoption as Sons of God*, 13–57.

39. Peppard, *Son of God in the Roman World*, 50–85.

40. This is a logical sequence of presenting the five passages on adoption based

1. The Authoring of Adoption: Ephesians 1:5

Ephesians 1:5 situates in the broader context of verses 3 to 14 in which the actions of the Triune God in planning and securing redemption delineate in a tripartite structure: vv. 3–6 describing the Father's work, vv. 7–12, the Son's, and vv. 13–14, the Spirit's. Besides, each section ends with the literary marker of a doxology: "to the praise of his glorious grace" (v. 6) and "to the praise of his glory" (v. 12, v. 14).

In vv. 4–5, Paul says, "Even as he chose us in him before the foundation of the world, that we should be holy and blameless before him. In love, he predestined us for *adoption* [υἱοθεσίαν] as sons through Jesus Christ, according to the purpose of his will." It is God the Father, Paul explicitly states, who purposes adoption. This adoption is not an afterthought but is God's predestined decree. The Greek word προορίσας means "decide upon beforehand, predetermine."[41] The timing of this predestination unto adoption is before the foundation of the world. This predestination, in turn, follows the choosing in Christ. Specifically, the Father predestines those who are chosen in Christ for adoption as sons. Moreover, this predestination is in love (ἐν ἀγάπῃ)—the steadfast love of God.

Significantly, the election is in (ἐν) Christ, but adoption is through (διά) Christ. It is "through [διά] his blood, the forgiveness of our trespasses" (v. 7) that God can adopt the elect as sons. Whereas the end of choosing is to be "holy and blameless," the means is by adoption. Besides, both election and predestination unto adoption are according to the purpose of the Father's will, not based on anything inherent in the elect.

The *telos* of the choosing and adoption as sons is "to the praise of his glorious grace" (v. 6), which is the doxological end of adoption. The broader context reveals that adoption is Trinitarian—God the Father authors adoption of the elect into his family (vv. 4–6), the Son redeems them (vv. 7–12), and the Spirit seals them to God's family (vv. 13–14), to the praise of the Triune God.

2. The Anticipation of Adoption: Romans 9:4

During the old covenant dispensation, God's pretemporal authoring of adoption unfolded in human history in typological fashion, in anticipation of the coming of the messiah. Adam, the first human being created by God

on redemptive history. A similar arrangement with different titles can be found in Trumper, "From Slaves to Sons."

41. "προορίσας," BDAG, 873.

in his image and likeness, was God's son (Luke 3:38) in the sense that God created him.[42] Moses, being a typology of Christ himself,[43] was an adopted son of Pharaoh's daughter (Exod 2:10).[44]

The most remarkable typological adoption, on a corporate scale, was the adoption of the nation of Israel (Deut 32:6). When the Israelites were still in Egypt, God called Israel his "firstborn son" (Exod 4:22–23), with all the attendant privileges of sonship. After the Israelites were out of Egypt at Mount Sinai, God gave them the law, regarded as the constitution of the nation, which also marked the official occasion when Israel was adopted.[45] This adoption was based on grace and set Israel apart as the apple of God's eye (Deut 32:9–12).

On a personal scale, sometimes individual Davidic kings are said to be God's sons (Ps 2:7; 89:26–27).[46] God promised to establish a house for David (2 Sam 7:11), and his son was called a son of God whom God would discipline when he sinned but would not cast him out like Saul (2 Sam 7:14–16).[47]

Paul, in Rom 9:3–5, says, "For I could wish that I myself were accursed and cut off from Christ for the sake of my brothers, my kinsmen according to the flesh. They are Israelites, and to them belong the *adoption* [υἱοθεσία], the glory, the covenants, the giving of the law, the worship, and the promises. To them belong the patriarchs, and from their race, according to the flesh, is the Christ, who is God over all, blessed forever. Amen." Adoption tops the list of eight exclusive privileges of Israelites, which culminate in Christ, the source of all blessings.[48]

Both Israel and the Davidic kings, however, had not been faithful. Israel, as an adopted son of God, had been perpetually disobedient (Hos 11:1–4; Pss 78, 106). The forty-year wandering in the wilderness for the exodus generation was considered a disciplinary action by God, wherein he says in Deut 8:5, "Know then in your heart that, as a man disciplines his son,

42. The phrase "image and likeness," argues Greg Beale, is characteristic of the language of sonship. Beale, *New Testament Biblical Theology*, 401.

43. A. W. Pink lists seventy-five markers that Moses foreshadows Christ. Pink, *Gleanings in Exodus*, 379–84.

44. Christ, in his human nature, being born of a woman without a human father, was adopted by Joseph (Matt 1:19–25), making him a son of David through Joseph's line. See Levin, "'Adoption' of Jesus."

45. Trumper, "From Slaves to Sons," 18.

46. Peterson, *Adopted by God*, 20–23.

47. This son is Solomon. God even renamed him Jedidiah, which means "beloved of God" (2 Sam 12:24–25).

48. The eight privileges listed in vv. 4–5 are adoption, the glory, the covenants, the giving of the law, the worship, the promises, the patriarchs, and, finally, Christ—the fountainhead of all blessings.

the LORD your God disciplines you." The subsequent Assyrian captivity and Babylon exile were also God's discipline for his disobedient son, Israel.

God's adoption of Israel, as revealed by her national history, had not achieved its intended purpose of making her "a kingdom of priests and a holy nation" (Exod 19:6). The Davidic kings, starting from David and Solomon, had not been entirely faithful either. The failure of Israel and the Davidic kings as adopted sons raised anticipation of a greater adopted Son, an Israelite himself and a son of David, to succeed where national Israel and the kings had failed.

3. The Arrival of Adoption: Galatians 4:4–5

Jesus Christ, the Messiah of God, has both a divine and a human nature. While his divine nature is eternal, without beginning and end, his human nature is only half-eternal, with a beginning but no end. When the fullness of time had come, says Paul in Gal 4:4–5, "God sent forth His Son, born of a woman, born under the Law, in order that [ἵνα] He might redeem those who were under the Law, that [ἵνα] we might receive the *adoption* [υἱοθεσίαν] as sons."[49]

The first ἵνα in v. 5 speaks to the fact that God's Son was born under the law to redeem those who were under the law. To accomplish this redemption, the Son, by being born under the law, is required to keep all the laws. This perfect keeping of the law provides the basis of justification in which Christ's righteousness imputes to the elect through the vehicle of faith. In the reverse direction, Jesus receives the imputation of the sins of the elect to himself for which God would punish him. Jesus would suffer a vicarious and substitutionary death for his people.

By virtue of Jesus' resurrection on the third day, God declared him to be "the Son of God in power according to the Spirit of holiness" (Rom 1:4). He was also the firstfruits of those who have fallen asleep (1 Cor 15:20) and the firstborn among many brothers (Rom 8:29). Christ, in his human nature, because of his resurrection, was adopted by God into his family to become the Elder Brother of all those who would be adopted later (Heb 2:10–13). Only then can the Spirit impart the adoptive benefits earned by the Son to the elect by uniting them to the Son through Spirit-engendered faith.

This redemption from the law, as explained by the second ἵνα in v. 5, is unto the purpose of receiving adoption as sons. As sons, God has sent the Spirit of his Son into the hearts of the redeemed, crying, "Abba! Father!" The

---

49. Here, the NASB version is used instead of the ESV version because the latter has not translated the first ἵνα at the beginning of verse 5.

arrival of God's Son made possible the arrival of adoption as sons through his redemption.

4. The Assurance of Adoption: Romans 8:15

Romans 8:15 depicts the present aspect of adoption: "For you did not receive the spirit of slavery to fall back into fear, but you have received the Spirit of adoption [πνεῦμα υἱοθεσίας] as sons, by whom we cry, 'Abba! Father!'" Here, Paul contrasts the spirit believers had before their adoption (spirit of slavery) and the Spirit they now have after their adoption (Spirit of adoption). Believers can cry "Abba! Father!" only by the presence of this Spirit of adoption. Chapter 5 will present a detailed exegetical-theological analysis of Rom 8:12–17, the core text of the assurance of adoption.

5. The Achievement of Adoption: Romans 8:23

The future aspect of adoption is the redemption of the body. It is the final achievement and consummation of adoption stated in Rom 8:23, which situates in the broader context of vv. 18–30 concerning the future glory of believers. This future glory, however, is preceded by present suffering (v. 18). The whole creation, due to this suffering, has been groaning together in the pains of childbirth (v. 22). The next verse reveals that not only the creation but also the believers, who have the firstfruits of the Spirit, groan as they wait eagerly for adoption as sons, the redemption of their bodies (v. 23). Here, the adoption as sons is equivalent to the redemption of the bodies, which will be realized when Christ comes the second time. This culminating adoption in v. 23 is in organic connection with the realized adoption in v. 15.[50] As is characteristic in Pauline eschatology, the future has invaded the present and is transforming the present due to the epochal success of Jesus' resurrection.

The concept of adoption, as indicated by this brief analysis of the fivefold usage of υἱοθεσία, spans the whole gamut of time: from before creation (Eph 1:4), to the period of old covenant dispensation (Rom 9:4), to the coming of the Messiah (Gal 4:4–5), to the present state of believers (Rom 8:15) under the new covenant, and finally to Christ's return (Rom 8:23) when the full benefits of adoption will come into fruition. In Paul's fivefold use of υἱοθεσία, as Tim Trumper puts it, we have "a sketch of the entire history of

---

50. Garner, *Sons in the Son*, 108.

redemption."[51] Table 2 outlines the significance, time frame, and theology of this fivefold usage of υἱοθεσία, which is inherently Christocentric.

Table 2: The significance of adoption and its correspondence with Christology

Scripture	Significance	Time Frame	Christology
Ephesians 1:5	The Authoring of Adoption	Eternity Past	Christ as the Eternal Logos
Romans 9:4	The Anticipation of Adoption	Old Testament Period	The Prefiguring of Christ
Galatians 4:4–5	The Arrival of Adoption	Between OT and NT	The Incarnation of Christ
Romans 8:15	The Assurance of Adoption	New Testament Period	The Death, Resurrection, Ascension, and Session of Christ
Romans 8:23	The Achievement of Adoption	Eternity Future	The Return of Christ

D. FURTHER ASPECTS OF ASSURANCE OF ADOPTION

The assurance of adoption does not make us God's children any more than the assurance of salvation makes us saved. It does, however, assure us that *we are* God's children, touching on the communal aspect of the adoption-centric understanding of assurance. God adopts many children, not only one child. He desires to bring many sons to glory, not only one son (Heb 2:10). Jesus is the Elder Brother of many brothers, not only one brother (Heb 2:11).

In the same vein, the language of Rom 8:14–17 is exclusively and conspicuously plural: *sons* of God (v. 14); by whom *we* cry, "Abba! Father!" (v. 15); the Spirit himself testifies with *our* spirit that *we are children* of God (v. 16); *children* are heirs provided *we* suffer with him in order that *we* may also glorify with him (v. 17). The focus is not "I am a child of God," but "we are children of God." It is when God's children, amid corporate instead of individual suffering, collectively cry out, "Abba, Father," that the Spirit testifies with believers' spirit that they are children of God. Corporate sonship is confirmed in the face of suffering when believers are groaning (v. 23) and the Spirit is also groaning with them (v. 26). This testimony of the Spirit with believers' spirit about their adoption forms another basis of assurance

51. Trumper, *History Teaches Us Nothing*, 85.

of salvation. This testimony is in addition to God's scriptural promises and the examination of the fruit of the Spirit.

This threefold basis of assurance is evident from the Westminster Confession of Faith (WCF) 18.2. There, the Westminster divines delineate the bases of assurance of salvation on three separate grounds. "The divine truth of the promises of salvation" is an objective ground of assurance based on God's scriptural revelation. "The inward evidence of those graces unto which these promises are made" is a predominantly subjective ground of assurance in examining the fruit of the Spirit.[52] "The testimony of the Spirit of adoption witnessing with our spirits that we are the children of God" is both an objective and a subjective ground of assurance based on the personal and immediate testifying of the Spirit in conjunction with believers' spirit. It is objective because it is the Spirit, the Third Person of the Trinity, who is testifying. It is subjective because it is also the believers' spirit who is testifying. These three grounds of assurance, John Frame rightly observes, correspond to the doctrines of justification, sanctification, and adoption, respectively.[53]

One can now see how instrumental the Spirit is in the ministry of assurance. Just as conversion involves the mind, the heart, and the will, so does assurance. Conversion entails the *mind* to understand one's sinfulness and God's provision of salvation in Jesus, the *heart* to feel the ugliness of sins and the beauty of the Savior, and the *will* to embrace Christ through Spirit-engendered faith. Likewise, in assurance, it is the Spirit, the Spirit of truth, who opens the *minds* of believers to convict them of the truthfulness of God's promises in Scripture concerning salvation (John 16:13). It is the Spirit, the Spirit of adoption, who testifies with the human spirit, in the *hearts* of believers, that they are children of God (Rom 8:15–16). It is the Spirit, the Spirit of sanctification, who produces the fruit of the Spirit (Gal 5:22–23) as believers resolve in their *wills* to be led by the Spirit to live according to the Spirit (Rom 8:12–14).

Assurance, therefore, is not merely an intellectual assent to some objective truth about salvation or a personal reflection. Neither is it merely an introspective examination of the fruits of a changed life. Assurance also involves a testimony in the heart by the Spirit, with the believers' spirit, that they are children of God. Both salvation and its assurance, then, involve the Spirit's work in the knowing, being, and doing of believers.

---

52. This examination includes both practical syllogism and mystical syllogism. The former entails examining the outward behavior changes in a person's life after conversion, the latter the inward spiritual growth of a person's Christlike character; see Beeke, "The Assurance Debate," 273–76.

53. Frame, *Systematic Theology*, 1003–7.

One can visualize assurance as a three-legged stool.[54] The ground of the stool is union with Christ because assurance, like any other benefit of redemption, flows from and builds on union with Christ. The three legs of the stool, doctrinally, correspond to justification, adoption, and sanctification. The Spirit, in his ministry of assurance, confirms to the minds, hearts, and wills of believers that they are children of God. From another perspective, justification, adoption, and sanctification are, respectively, the foundation, confirmation, and cultivation of assurance.

The three legs, ethically, correspond to the theological virtues of faith, hope, and love, respectively. This is because justification is by faith, which comes from the hearing of God's words (Rom 10:17). Adoption is by the sure hope (ἐλπίς) that a person is a child of God now and forever. Sanctification manifests in growing in love toward God and one's neighbors.[55]

All three legs of assurance, focusing on the word, prayer, and fruit, are essential and complementary to one another. Believers should not accentuate one leg at the expense of the other two. A justification-centric view of assurance focuses on the doctrinal understanding of God's promises of forgiveness of sins for those who trust in Jesus as their Savior and Lord. Still, it should not exclude the conviction of the heart and the fruit of the Spirit. An adoption-centric understanding of assurance stresses the testimony of the Spirit in the heart. However, it does not belittle the basic knowledge of the gospel and turn a blind eye on the evidence of a changed life. A sanctification-centric understanding of assurance looks at the fruits of the believers. Nevertheless, it does not neglect knowledge of the fundamental truths of salvation and a heartfelt trust in God as the Heavenly Father.

Though all the three legs are essential, adoption, as this study has shown, most comprehensively captures the theological richness of salvation.[56] The figure visualizes assurance as a three-legged stool.

54. The illustration of assurance as a three-legged stool can be found in Schreiner and Caneday, *Race Set Before Us*, 276, yet the analysis in this study is vastly different.

55. Love is the first element listed in the fruit of the Spirit (Gal 5:22). It is *the* virtue that binds all virtues together (Col 3:14).

56. For understanding how the traditional *ordo salutis* is modified for viewing adoption, rather than justification or sanctification, as the inclusive benefit, see Garner, *Sons in the Son*, 301–11.

Assurance visualized as a three-legged stool.

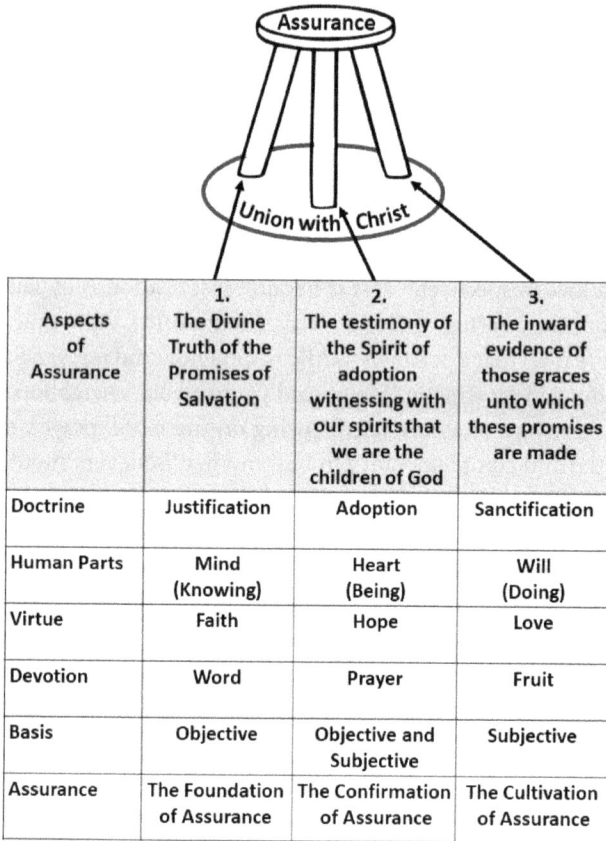

Aspects of Assurance	1. The Divine Truth of the Promises of Salvation	2. The testimony of the Spirit of adoption witnessing with our spirits that we are the children of God	3. The inward evidence of those graces unto which these promises are made
Doctrine	Justification	Adoption	Sanctification
Human Parts	Mind (Knowing)	Heart (Being)	Will (Doing)
Virtue	Faith	Hope	Love
Devotion	Word	Prayer	Fruit
Basis	Objective	Objective and Subjective	Subjective
Assurance	The Foundation of Assurance	The Confirmation of Assurance	The Cultivation of Assurance

E. ASSURANCE OF ADOPTION AND ASSURANCE OF CHRIST

Claiming assurance as adoption-centric does not negate the Christocentric nature of it. Assurance, like everything else in the Christian life, centers on Christ. Assurance, at its heart, is an assurance of Christ himself, not about receiving his benefits like justification or sanctification, not even adoption.

The Christocentric nature of assurance is especially poignant because assurance flows from and finds its basis in union with Christ. It is Christ (the benefactor) who is central, not Christians (the beneficiaries) or the gifts of salvation (the benefits). At its core, assurance is about Christ himself, not merely a union with him.

Assurance is, therefore, wholly Christological. Nevertheless, a statement like "assurance of Christ is assurance of salvation," though biblically and theologically sound, would be too broad and hardly need any justification. It adds little to what most Christians already know, which is, Christ should be believers' all in all. Christianity is about Christ, as most Christians would agree. He is "the founder and perfecter of our faith" (Heb 12:2). All theology, in a broad sense, is Christology.

As such, by arguing for an adoption-centric understanding of salvation, it does not pit against, much less negate, the Christocentricity of assurance. Instead, it brings a sharper focus on adoption, which, with its fivefold dimensions spanning from past to future eternity, most comprehensively captures the theological richness of salvation.

F. IS ASSURANCE OF THE ESSENCE OF FAITH?

If salvation is understood narrowly as justification, then assurance is of the essence of faith because faith involves trusting in "the divine truth of the promises of salvation." Assurance, in this case, is objective because God's promises are objective. However, if one understands salvation in the broader sense of comprising not merely justification but also adoption and sanctification and all the other elements in the *ordo salutis*, then assurance is not of faith's essence. This is because some of those other elements of salvation contain subjective appropriation of feelings and experiences, which vary from person to person and even within the same person at different times.

With an adoption-centric understanding of assurance, the answer to the question is "yes" and "no." Assurance is of the essence of faith because it is the Spirit who testifies to believers they are children of God. It is not entirely of faith's essence because it is also believers' spirit that testifies, and this testimony can vacillate at times. Chapter 5 will analyze this testimony at length.

G. SUMMARY

Assurance of salvation is a redemptive benefit flowing from union with Christ. Adoption is the highest and most comprehensive benefit encompassing the existential, judicial, relational, moral, and eschatological dimensions of salvation. Paul's fivefold use of adoption spans the whole gamut of redemption from eternity past to eternity future. An adoption-centric understanding of assurance best captures the theological depth and riches of salvation. In Part II, we shall approach assurance from a historical perspective.

PART II

Historical Analysis

Chapter 3

Assurance in History

The doctrine of assurance was not extensively debated in the early centuries in the patristic period due to preoccupation with other more fundamental theological issues such as Trinity and Christology.[1] No record is found, in fact, of Augustine's teaching on assurance. Only in the Middle Ages and the Reformation period did more discourses on assurance emerge as part of the broader discussions on soteriology.

This chapter, as such, only surveys the views of selective theologians on the doctrine of assurance, starting with Thomas Aquinas. Since an adoption-centric understanding of assurance is a new theological paradigm, the goal of this chapter is not so much to trace its development or defend it from history. Instead, the purpose is to provide a historical foundation on how theologians have understood assurance, especially on whether it is intrinsic to faith.

A. A BRIEF HISTORICAL SURVEY OF ASSURANCE OF SALVATION

1. Thomas Aquinas (1225–74)

Aquinas, in a section of his *magnum opus Summa Theologiae*, postulates that one could understand assurance through the three means of knowledge:

1. Letham, "Saving Faith and Assurance," 5–6.

33

revelation, deduction, and induction.[2] Aquinas's understanding of assurance is thus knowledge-centric. God can, on rare occasions, grant knowledge of assurance to a person through special revelation. Such scarce, direct revelation from God, argues Aquinas, encourages the person to "carry out remarkable tasks more confidently and courageously and endure the evils of this present life."[3] Besides, a person can gain knowledge of assurance through deductive reasoning from a known premise, which, Aquinas contends, is the foundation of God's grace. Since this foundation is God himself, who cannot be known exhaustively, Aquinas concludes that no one could have the assurance of salvation by deduction. Lastly, one can obtain knowledge of assurance via inductive reasoning from observing the fruits in a believer's life. The believer may conclude, based on these fruits, whether he or she has salvation. This assurance, however, could be misguided or even mistaken because the induction may be incomplete or inaccurate.

In conclusion, except in the rarest occasions by way of a direct revelation from God, absolute assurance of salvation, Aquinas contends, is unattainable. Most believers at best can obtain a small, incomplete measure of assurance through evaluating their lives via inductive reasoning. Assurance to Aquinas, therefore, is not of the essence of saving faith.

Aquinas's knowledge-centric understanding of assurance guided the Roman Catholic teaching on this topic in subsequent centuries down through the Reformation. The Reformers, of course, vehemently opposed this understanding. Around the time of Luther's death, the Council of Trent (1545–63) summarized the official Roman Catholic teaching on assurance. Assurance of salvation, as codified in the twelfth chapter of the Decree of Justification, is nearly impossible because to be assured of one's salvation is to know the mind of God in predestination.[4] The council says:

> No one, moreover, so long as he is in this mortal life, ought so far to presume as regards the secret mystery of divine predestination, as to determine for certain that he is assuredly in the number of the predestinate; as if it were true, that he that is justified, either cannot sin any more, or, if he does sin, that he ought to promise himself an assured repentance; for except by special revelation, it cannot be known whom God hath chosen unto Himself.[5]

---

2. The chapter is entitled "Can a Man Know That He Has Grace?" from Aquinas, *Summa Theologiae*, I-II.112.5.

3. Aquinas, *Summa Theologiae*, I-II.112.5.

4. Schaff, *Creeds of Christendom*, 2:103.

5. Schaff, *Creeds of Christendom*, 2:103.

The council also states, "No one can know with the certainty of faith, which excludes the possibility of error, that he continues in the grace of God."[6] Besides, "if any man holds trust, confidence, or assurance of pardon to be essential to faith, let him be accursed."[7] In effect, by the time of the Council of Trent, Aquinas's knowledge-centric understanding of assurance had evolved, over three centuries, into an election-centric understanding of assurance.

Assurance, from a Roman Catholic point of view, is unattainable because believers can neither guarantee they would never sin nor would they repent in the event of such future sins. This understanding of assurance is inseparable from Rome's understanding of salvation itself. Undoubtedly, if salvation is a synergy of God's grace and human's meritorious works, one can never be sure about the quality and quantity of the good works, which are indispensable to salvation.

2. Martin Luther (1483–1546)

Luther is no stranger to the doubt of salvation. His doctrine of assurance stems not so much from refuting the Roman Catholic position as from his own intense personal struggles with assurance. The Catholic Church, Luther aptly observes, not only discourages assurance but encourages doubt.[8] The latent fear of Rome, of course, was the illegitimate use of assurance as a license to live licentiously.

The Catholic teaching on assurance fueled Luther's great agony over the state of his soul. Luther, as were most believers brought up in the Roman Catholic system, was routinely tortured by doubts and did not have the joy of salvation. On certain occasions, when severe doubts assaulted him, he even resorted to asserting his status: "I am baptized."[9]

The turning point was his fresh discovery of the meaning of righteousness in Rom 1:16–17—righteousness does not pertain to the human effort of attaining it but the divine provision of it. After recovering the doctrine of justification by grace alone, through faith alone, in Christ alone, Luther learned to cling to the promises of God in Christ as an objective basis of his assurance.

Luther categorically rejects the Catholic Church's teaching on assurance. He writes:

6. Stoeffler, "Wesleyan Concept of Religious Certainty," 132.

7. Wesley, *Works of John Wesley*, 8:23.

8. Luther, "Lectures on Genesis 21–25," 145.

9. Luther, quoted in Pfürtner, *Luther and Aquinas*, 149–50.

We must daily more and more endeavor to destroy at the root that pernicious error (that man cannot know whether or not he is in a state of grace), by which the whole world is seduced. If we doubt God's grace and do not believe that God is well-pleased in us for Christ's sake, then we are denying that Christ has redeemed us—indeed, we question outright all his benefits.[10]

Luther conceives of three grounds of assurance.[11] The primary one is the truthful character of God, who has made promises that whosoever believes in Christ will receive eternal life (John 3:16). Besides, believers are sure nothing will separate them from the love of God (Rom 8:31–39). Such is the objective ground of assurance, the basis of which is the immutability of God. Luther writes in his *Bondage of the Will*:

Since God has taken my salvation out of my hands into his, making it depend on his choice and not mine, and has promised to save me, not by my own work and exertion but by his grace and mercy, I am assured and certain both that he is faithful and will not lie to me, and also that he is too great and powerful for any demons or any adversities to be able to break him or to snatch me from him.[12]

The second ground of assurance is an obedient lifestyle resultant from saving faith. A changed life marked by obedience to God's commands provides circumstantial evidence a person is a child of God. Luther points to "the Keys, Baptism, and the Eucharist" as the secondary means of assurance.[13] In Luther's thinking, there is a positive cycle of mutual reinforcement between assurance and obedience in which assurance promotes obedience, which further fosters assurance.

The third ground of assurance is objective but with a subjective appropriation. This ground is the testimony from the Holy Spirit, who convinces the believer of God's saving grace. Luther writes, "It is a right and sure Spirit who . . . does not allow us to doubt but carries out what Paul admonishes: 'Let everyone be fully convinced in his own mind' (Rom 14:5)."[14]

In short, Luther, for apparent reasons, adopts a justification-centric understanding of assurance, but not to the exclusion of the fruits of sanctification and the testimony of the Spirit of adoption.

10. Pfürtner, *Luther and Aquinas*, 120.
11. Hoskinson, *Assurance of Salvation*, 26.
12. Luther, *Basic Theological Writings*, 220.
13. Hoskinson, *Assurance of Salvation*, 28.
14. Luther, "Lectures on Genesis 38–44," 154.

3. John Calvin (1509–64)

Calvin, like Luther, also rejects the view of Rome on assurance. While Luther stresses the word of God as the objective ground of assurance, Calvin emphasizes the work of the Spirit. "It was Calvin more than anyone else," contends Robert Letham, "who was responsible for the emergence of the doctrine of the internal testimony of the Holy Spirit and for stressing that it was this that was the root cause of all assurance that the Christian enjoyed."[15]

For Calvin, the testimony of the Spirit is not separate from Scripture because the Spirit, after having illuminated the minds of the believers, also seals the promises of Scripture to the hearts of believers to assure them the truthfulness of God's words.[16] This work of the Spirit provides both the objective and subjective grounds of assurance in the sequence below:

> For first, the Lord teaches and instructs us by his Word. Secondly, he confirms it by the sacraments. Finally, he illumines our minds by the light of his Holy Spirit and opens our hearts for the Word and sacraments to enter in, which would otherwise only strike our ears and appear before our eyes, but not at all affect us within.[17]

Calvin's understanding of assurance derives from his Trinitarian understanding of saving faith, of which he famously writes:

> Now we shall possess a right definition of faith if we call it a firm and certain knowledge of God's benevolence toward us, founded upon the truth of the freely given promise in Christ, both revealed to our minds and sealed upon our hearts through the Holy Spirit.[18]

Assurance is thus tethered to saving faith, which is a sure knowledge of the Father's favor, founded on the free promise in the Son, and revealed to the minds and sealed to the hearts by the Spirit. Because saving faith is a firm and sure knowledge of the divine grace, in Calvin's mind, assurance and faith are inseparable or, in other words, assurance is of the essence of saving faith.[19] Calvin defines the nature of assurance as follows:

> Briefly, he alone is truly a believer who, convinced by a firm conviction that God is a kindly and well-disposed Father toward

15. Letham, "Saving Faith and Assurance," 20–21.
16. Calvin, *Institutes*, 3.2.36 (583–84).
17. Calvin, *Institutes*, 4.14.8 (1284).
18. Calvin, *Institutes*, 3.2.7 (551).
19. Hoskinson, *Assurance of Salvation*, 32–34.

him, promises himself all things on the basis of his generosity; who, relying upon the promises of divine benevolence toward him, lays hold on an undoubted expectation of salvation.[20]

Assurance, based on Calvin's language, is a mark of a true believer!

Calvin also considers the doctrine of predestination as an integral part of assurance. "Predestination, rightly understood," Calvin notes, "brings no shaking of faith but rather its best confirmation."[21] Predestination thus buttresses assurance as it accentuates both salvation and perseverance as of grace and not of works.[22]

Calvin, in the end, comes to the same conclusion as Luther regarding the means of assurance. It entails the promises of God in Christ, the obedient lifestyle of the believer, and the testimony of the Holy Spirit, with the first being more objective than the other two.[23]

In the final analysis, however, Calvin's understanding of assurance is best described as Spirit-centric because it is the Spirit who reveals to the minds and seals to the hearts of believers the promise of salvation in Christ. Assurance, in other words, is a ministry of the Holy Spirit.

4. William Perkins (1558–1602)

Perkins, regarded by some as the father of English Puritanism, was a towering theologian in the sixteenth century.[24] His conception of assurance, as with most other theologians, flows from his understanding of saving faith. He writes:

> Whereas some are of opinion, that faith is an affiance or confidence, that seems to be otherwise: for it is a fruit of faith, and indeed no man can put any confidence in God, till he be first of all persuaded of God's mercy in Christ towards him.[25]

Perkins views assurance as a fruit of faith. Therefore, there has been a decisive shift in emphasis, however subtle, from the content of faith to its effect. Since fruit varies in quantity and quality from person to person, assurance is not of the essence of faith for Perkins.

20. Calvin, *Institutes*, 3.2.16 (562).

21. Calvin, *Institutes*, 3.24.9 (975–76).

22. Calvin, *Institutes*, 3.21.1 (920–23).

23. Hoskinson, *Assurance of Salvation*, 39.

24. Beeke, *Living for God's Glory*, 295.

25. Perkins, *Works of William Perkins*, 1:125.

Assuredly, Perkins distinguishes between weak and strong faith, with the latter being "a full persuasion of the mercy of God," which could only be attained after some time has elapsed, after "keeping a good conscience," and after having had many experiences of God's favor.[26] Perkins, to put it otherwise, regards assurance as not indispensable from saving faith and will come only after a protracted period in those whose faith is mature and developed.

Perkins, as such, considers assurance as something to be obtained after self-examination and in conjunction with holy living, the cultivation of Christian virtues, and the use of the means of grace.[27] It is thus a sanctification-centric understanding of assurance. Perkins's view on assurance emerged out of his pastoral concern for those who feared whether they were among God's elect.[28] Many Puritan pastors also shared similar pastoral concerns as Perkin.[29]

5. John Wesley (1703–91)

While both Luther and Calvin base assurance on God's promises, believers' obedient lifestyle, and testimony of the Spirit, Wesley only accentuates the latter two as the means of assurance.[30] Assurance, based on his two published sermons on Rom 8:16 in 1746 and 1767, comes from the dual means of the witness of the Holy Spirit and the testimony of one's spirit.[31] The witness of the Spirit is the primary basis of assurance in which the Spirit assures believers they are "in Christ":

> It is also the office of the Holy Ghost, to "assure us of the adoption of sons," to create in us a sense of the paternal love of God toward us, to give us an earnest of our everlasting inheritance.[32]

This Spirit's witnessing, on the one hand, concerns the adoption of believers as God's children. Wesley, in a sermon preached in 1746 on Rom 8:16, asserts:

> The Spirit of God does give a believer such a testimony of his adoption, that while it is present to the soul, he can no more

26. Perkins, *Works of William Perkins*, 1:366–67.
27. Perkins, *Works of William Perkins*, 2:18–21.
28. Perkins, *Works of William Perkins*, 1:421.
29. Letham, "Saving Faith and Assurance," 54.
30. Hoskinson, *Assurance of Salvation*, 45.
31. Noll, "John Wesley and Assurance," 167.
32. Wesley, *Works of John Wesley*, 8:100.

doubt the reality of his sonship than he can doubt of the shining of the sun, while he stands in the full blaze of his beams.[33]

The testimony of the believer's spirit, on the other hand, involves a combination of "revelation, experience, and simple logic."[34] In Wesley's own words: "an examination of ourselves that we do love God and seek to please him is the witness of our spirit."[35] This means of assurance is equivalent to examining the obedient lifestyle of the believer as evidence of salvation. The witnessing of the Spirit, therefore, is not independent of the fruit of the Spirit. Wesley says:

> Nor do we assert, that there can be any real testimony of the Spirit without the fruit of the Spirit. We assert on the contrary, that the fruit of the Spirit immediately springs from this testimony.[36]

Wesley's conception of assurance, however, is restricted to a confidence of the present salvation only because he rejects the doctrine of the perseverance of the saints.[37] A believer, Wesley maintains, can have "*a present* assurance of *present* salvation and never a *present* assurance of *final* salvation."[38] Hence, despite his emphasis on an obedient lifestyle and the testimony of the Spirit, Wesley's understanding of assurance is, ironically, perseverance-centric because believers can only be assured of their present salvation as long as they persevere in their sanctification and adoption.

B. IS ASSURANCE OF THE ESSENCE OF FAITH?

The answer to this question depends on the theologian. For Thomas Aquinas, the answer is a resounding "no" because he holds to a knowledge-centric understanding of assurance in which only the rarest few may gain the specialized knowledge of their salvation. For Martin Luther and John Calvin, whose view of assurance is justification-centric and Spirit-centric, the answer is "yes" as they both ground assurance on the objective basis of God's scriptural promises revealed through the Spirit. Assurance, for William Perkins, is not intrinsic to faith because assurance is sanctification-centric. One

---

33. Wesley, *Wesley's Standard Sermons*, 1:210.

34. Noll, "John Wesley and Assurance," 168.

35. Wesley, *Wesley's Standard Sermons*, 1:289.

36. Wesley, *Wesley's Standard Sermons*, 2:346.

37. Hoskinson, *Assurance of Salvation*, 48.

38. Noll, "John Wesley and Assurance," 164.

can never be sure whether the quality and the quantity of the fruits are good enough. For John Wesley, assurance is of the essence of a present faith but not of a future one because assurance is perseverance-centric. Table 3 summarizes the response of the theologians.

Table 3: Is assurance of the essence of faith for the theologians?

Theologians	View of Assurance	Is Assurance of the Essence of Faith?
Thomas Aquinas	Knowledge-centric	No
Martin Luther	Justification-centric	Yes
John Calvin	Spirit-centric	Yes
William Perkins	Sanctification-centric	No
John Wesley	Perseverance-centric	Yes for present salvation. No for future salvation.

C. SUMMARY

Based on this brief historical analysis of the different conceptions of assurance, a person's understanding of assurance is shaped not only by his theology of salvation (or saving faith) but also by the historical forces and personal circumstances in which the theologians find themselves. None of the theologians surveyed, however, have centered assurance squarely in the context of adoption. In the next chapter, we will examine the view of assurance not of individual theologians but of committees of divines who drafted the confessional statements of the Reformed churches.

Chapter 4

Assurance in Reformed Catechisms and Confessions

In the sixteenth and seventeenth centuries, churches, on the one hand, needed to define their theology with other communions and cities and towns, and, on the other hand, wanted to define themselves relative to each other. These dual currents of theology and politics facilitated the creation of many Protestant confessions and catechisms.[1]

Among the various confessions and catechisms produced, the Anglican Articles in Anglican churches,[2] the Scots Confession in Scottish churches,[3] the Book of Concord in Lutheran churches,[4] the Three Forms of Unity in Dutch Reformed churches,[5] the Westminster Standards in Presby-

---

1. Trueman, *Creedal Imperative*, 109.

2. The Anglican Articles consist of the Book of Common Prayer (1549), the Thirty-Nine Articles (1571), and the Homilies (1547, 1571).

3. The Scots Confession of 1560 was drafted by John Knox and five other Scotsmen (John Willock, John Winram, John Spottiswoode, John Douglas, and John Row).

4. The Book of Concord is a collection of Lutheran confessional documents and was adopted in 1580.

5. The Three Forms of Unity include the Belgic Confession (1561), the Heidelberg Catechism (1563), and the Canons of Dort (1619).

terian churches,[6] and the Baptist Confession in Baptist churches[7] have had the most impact on Protestantism.[8] The goal of this chapter is to compare the doctrine of assurance between the Heidelberg Catechism (HC), under the Three Forms of Unity, and the Westminster Confession of Faith (WCF), under the Westminster Standards.

A. HEIDELBERG CATECHISM (HC)

Elector Frederick III (1515–76), also known as "the Pious" of the Palatinate, initiated the creation of the HC. In the early 1560s in the city of Heidelberg, the capital of the Palatinate region in Germany, Frederick the Pious feared the circulation of catechisms of different theological leanings might endanger the transmission of the central doctrines of Christianity to the next generation and erode the unity of the faith.[9] In 1562, he recruited a young theologian, Zacharias Ursinus (1534–83), at the University of Heidelberg. Ursinus, along with his young assistant preacher, Caspar Olevianus (1536–87), and other scholars at the university, drafted the influential HC.

This cooperation of a professor and a pastor, who were the brain and heart of the HC, gave the unique "blend of theological depth and pastoral warmth" for which the HC is most famous.[10] The HC was officially adopted in January 1563 by a Heidelberg synod and was quickly translated into Latin and Dutch, and later into French and English.[11] The Synod of Dort approved the HC in 1618–19.[12]

The HC, in the mind of Elector Frederick III, would serve three objectives: "as a catechetical tool for teaching the children; as a preaching guide for instructing the common people in the churches; and as a form for confessional unity among the several Protestant factions in the Palatinate."[13] The content of the HC was based mainly on Ursinus's own Smaller Catechism

6. The Westminster Standards is a collection of documents drawn up by the Westminster Assembly (1643–48), consisting of the Directory of Public Worship (1645), the Form of Church Government (1645), the Westminster Confession of Faith (1647), the Westminster Shorter Catechism (1647), and the Westminster Larger Catechism (1648).

7. The Baptist Confession published in 1689 is based on the Westminster Confession of Faith with modifications to reflect the Baptist view on baptism and church polity.

8. Trueman, *Creedal Imperative*, 110.

9. Barrett, *Heidelberg Catechism*, 19.

10. Bierma, *Introduction to Heidelberg Catechism*, 52.

11. Barrett, *Heidelberg Catechism*, 23.

12. *Ecumenical Creeds and Reformed Confessions*, 12.

13. Bierma, *Introduction to Heidelberg Catechism*, 51.

(1561) and, to a lesser extent, his Larger Catechism (1562).[14] The theology of the HC accentuated the commonality between Lutheran and Reformed churches while avoiding, except for the teaching concerning Eucharist, most of the controversies dividing them.[15] The creation of the HC, in the view of some, was a response to the Council of Trent.[16]

The HC consists of 129 questions and answers divided into fifty-two sections called "Lord's Day," intended as sermon materials to be preached on each Sunday of the year. The salient characteristic of the HC is its presentation of the Christian doctrines from the vantage point of personal and practical Christian living instead of abstract theological formulations. Another well-known feature of the HC is the arrangement of all its 129 questions in a tri-partite structure commonly summarized by "Guilt, Grace, and Gratitude" or "Sin, Salvation, and Service."[17] This partition comes from the answer to Q. 2.[18]

> Q. 2: What do you need to know in order to live and die in the joy of this comfort?

> A. 2: First, how great my sins and misery are;[1] second, how I am deliv-ered from all my sins and misery;[2] third, how I am to be thankful to God for such deliverance.[3][19]

This threefold structure patterns after the book of Romans. Part 1 deals with "Human Misery" or "Guilt" because of sin (Q. 3–11, Rom 1:1—3:20). Part 2 presents "Human Deliverance" or "Grace" through grace in Christ (Q. 12–85, Rom 3:21—11:36). Part 3 covers the "Response" or "Gratitude" of the redeemed in living out the Christian life (Q. 86–129, Rom 12–16).[20]

B. WESTMINSTER CONFESSION OF FAITH (WCF)

Three generations after the creation of the HC, the English Long Parliament, in observing the Solemn League and Covenant, appointed the Westminster Assembly to advise on the reformation of the church in England against

---

14. Bierma, *Introduction to Heidelberg Catechism*, 15.

15. Barrett, *Heidelberg Catechism*, 24.

16. Hazlett, "Reformed Theology in Confessions," 194.

17. Boekestein, *Quest for Comfort*, 20.

18. Q. 1 and Q. 2 of the HC introduce the overall theme and the structure of the HC.

19. [1] Rom 3:9–10; 1 John 1:10. [2] John 17:3; Acts 4:12; 10:43. [3] Matt 5:16; Rom 6:13; Eph 5:8–10; 1 Pet 2:9–10.

20. Bierma, *Theology of Heidelberg Catechism*, 30–31.

"tyranny, popery, and Arminianism."[21] As a result, the Westminster Standards (1643–48), consisting of the WCF (1647) along with the accompanying Westminster Shorter Catechism (1647) and Larger Catechism (1648), were created during the meeting of the Westminster Assembly (1643–48) at Westminster Abbey during the English Civil Wars.[22]

The purpose of the assembly was to bring the Church of England into closer conformity of faith and practice with the Presbyterian Church of Scotland and other Reformed churches.[23] The divines who produced the WCF consisted of scholars, pastors, and theologians from various constituents from England and Scotland.[24] Specifically, there were four types of divines working with the Scottish commissioners to produce the WCF:[25]

1. Moderate Episcopalians (e.g., Dr. Ussher)

2. Independents (e.g., Puritan Thomas Goodwin)

3. Erastians (e.g., Dr. John Lightfoot)

4. Presbyterians (e.g., Matthew Newcomen)

In terms of the content, the WCF consists of thirty-three chapters in the following five sections:[26]

1. Chapters I–V   God, his word, being, and works

2. Chapters VI–XVIII   Man, sin, and restoration through Christ

3. Chapters XIX–XXIV   God's law, man's liberties, and duties

4. Chapters XXV–XXXI   The church, fellowship, and ordinances

5. Chapters XXXII–XXXIII The last things

The teachings of the WCF encompass all branches of systematic theology: bibliology and theology proper (section 1); theological anthropology, Christology, and soteriology (section 2); ethics and practical theology (section 3); ecclesiology (section 4); and eschatology (section 5). Sinclair Ferguson describes the theology of the WCF as "Calvinistic in emphasis, Federal in its basic structure, and Evangelical in its view of the relationship between God and man."[27]

21. Torrance, "Westminster Theology," 41.
22. Letham, *Westminster Assembly*, 1.
23. Gerstner et al., *Westminster Confession of Faith*, vii.
24. Beeke and Ferguson, *Reformed Confessions Harmonized*, xii.
25. Torrance, "Westminster Theology," 40.
26. Ferguson, "Teaching of the Confession, 28.
27. Ferguson, "Teaching of the Confession, 29.

By "Calvinistic," it underscores the sovereignty and eternal decrees of God, especially as they relate to the predestination of the elect in Christ from before the foundation of the world to be the beneficiaries of Christ's saving grace. By "federal theology," it refers to two covenants.[28] The covenant of works is God's covenant with Adam as the federal head of humanity, promising eternal life to man upon perfect obedience.[29] The covenant of grace is God's covenant with Christ, the second Adam, as the federal head of the new humanity. In this second covenant, Christ keeps the original covenant with Adam, bears the penalty for breaking it, and, through the Holy Spirit, applies his redemptive work to the elect.[30] By "evangelical," it refers to the preaching of the doctrines of grace and their applications to believers. Even to date, the WCF epitomizes the culmination of the theology of English Puritanism in confessional form.

C. ASSURANCE OF SALVATION IN HC

In the HC, the most famous Q. 1 embeds the topic of assurance.

Q. 1: What is your only comfort in life and death?

A. 1: That I am not my own,[1] but belong with body and soul, both in life and in death,[2] to my faithful Saviour Jesus Christ.[3] He has fully paid for all my sins with His precious blood,[4] and has set me free from all the power of the devil.[5] He also preserves me in such a way[6] that without the will of my Heavenly Father not a hair can fall from my head;[7] indeed, all things must work together for my salvation. [8] Therefore, *by His Holy Spirit He also assures me of eternal life*[9] and makes me heartily willing and ready from now on to live for Him.[10][31]

A believer's *only* comfort in life and death is that "I am not my own," but rather, belong entirely and eternally to Jesus. This answer introduces

---

28. For the origin and history of the development of federal theology, see Weir, *Origins of Federal Theology*.

29. The covenant of works is covered in WCF 7.2 on "God's covenant with man" and WCF 19.1 and 19.6 on "the Law of God."

30. The covenant of grace is covered in WCF 7.3 and 7.4 on "God's covenant with man," WCF 14.2 on "saving faith," WCF 17.2 on "perseverance of the saints," WCF 27.1 on "the sacraments," and WCF 28.1 on "baptism."

31. [1] 1 Cor 6:19–20. [2] Rom 14:7–9. [3] 1 Cor 3:23; Titus 2:14. [4] 1 Pet 1:18–19; 1 John 1:7; 2:2. [5] John 8:34–36; Heb 2:14–15; 1 John 3:8. [6] John 6:39–40; 10:27–30; 2 Thess 3:3; 1 Pet 1:5. [7] Matt 10:29–31; Luke 21:16–18. [8] Rom 8:28. [9] Rom 8:15–16; 2 Cor 1:21–22; 5:5; Eph 1:13–14. [10] Rom 8:14.

the notion of comfort as an organizing theme for the entire document.[32] This comfort, for all practical purposes, is synonymous with assurance—in fact, *personal* assurance—due to the use of the first-person singular pronoun throughout the response. The Holy Spirit, by "[assuring] me of eternal life," provides that comfort. Significantly, the writers of the HC desire each believer to obtain assurance at the very outset of the catechism.

According to HC Q. and A. 53, this comfort, and thus assurance, is based on the work of the Holy Spirit.

Q. 53: What do you believe concerning the Holy Spirit?

A. 53: First, He is, together with the Father and the Son, true and eternal God.[1] Second, He is also given to me,[2] to make me by true faith share in Christ and all His benefits,[3] to *comfort* me,[4] and to remain with me forever.[5][33]

The Spirit provides a *present* assurance of *present* salvation by making believers partake in Christ and his benefits and by comforting them. Besides, according to HC Q. and A. 52, 57, and 58, this comfort is also eschatological:

Q. 52: What comfort is it to you that Christ will come to judge the living and the dead?

A. 52: In all my sorrow and persecution I lift up my head and eagerly await as the judge from heaven the very same person who before has submitted Himself to the judgment of God for my sake, and has removed all the curse from me.[1] He will cast all His and my enemies into everlasting condemnation, but *He will take me and all His chosen ones to Himself into heavenly joy and glory.*[2][34]

Q. 57: What comfort does the resurrection of the body offer you?

A. 57: Not only shall my soul *after this life* immediately be taken up to Christ, my Head,[1] but also this my flesh, raised by the power of Christ, shall be reunited with my soul and made like Christ's glorious body.[2][35]

32. Bierma, *Theology of Heidelberg Catechism*, 13.

33. [1] Gen 1:1–2; Matt 28:19; Acts 5:3–4; 1 Cor 3:16. [2] 1 Cor 6:19; 2 Cor 1:21–22; Gal 4:6; Eph 1:13. [3] Gal 3:14; 1 Pet 1:2. [4] John 15:26; Acts 9:31. [5] John 14:16–17; 1 Pet 4:14.

34. [1] Luke 21:28; Rom 8:22–25; Phil 3:20–21; Titus 2:13–14. [2] Matt 25:31–46; 1 Thess 4:16–17; 2 Thess 1:6–10.

35. [1] Luke 16:22; 23:43; Phil 1:21–23. [2] Job 19:25, 26; 1 Cor 15:20, 42–46, 54; Phil 3:21; 1 John 3:2.

Q. 58: What comfort do you receive from the article about life everlasting?

A. 58: Since I now already feel in my heart the beginning of eternal joy,[1] I shall *after this life* possess perfect blessedness, such as no eye has seen, nor ear heard, nor the heart of man conceived—a blessedness in which to praise God forever.[2]36

This comfort stems from a *present* assurance of *future* salvation by which the believer, at the *parousia*, will receive the consummation of salvation in heavenly joy and glory (A. 52), the resurrection of the body (A. 57), and perfect blessedness (A. 58).

Out of the 129 questions, Q. and A. 21 more directly embody the topic of assurance.

Q. 21: What is true faith?

A. 21: True faith is a sure knowledge whereby I accept as true all that God has revealed to us in His Word.[1] At the same time it is *a firm confidence*[2] that not only to others, but also to me,[3] *God has granted forgiveness of sins, everlasting righteousness, and salvation,*[4] out of mere grace, only for the sake of Christ's merits.[5] This faith the Holy Spirit works in my heart by the gospel.[6]37

Many characteristics of true faith, according to this definition, relate to believers' assurance. True faith is knowledge, not a feeling. It is not only knowledge but a *sure* knowledge, one with personal conviction. The content of that knowledge is God's revelation because true faith is "a sure knowledge whereby I accept as true all that God has revealed to us in His Word." Assurance of salvation, hence, has an objective basis in the sure knowledge of God's words and the truthfulness thereof. The origin of this faith is external to the believers as it emanates from God's revelation (Rom 10:17).[38] The specific content of God's word regarding salvation is "forgiveness of sins, everlasting righteousness, and salvation." True faith is a "firm confidence" in that knowledge. As a result, assurance of salvation is a definite confidence in the same knowledge.

This true faith is personal because it is a firm confidence "not only to others, but also *to me*." Belief in God's promises, consequently, is "not only belief in their truth, but it must include the belief that they are true

---

36. [1] John 17:3; Rom 14:17; 2 Cor 5:2–3. [2] John 17:24; 1 Cor 2:9.

37. [1] John 17:3, 17; Heb 11:1–3; Jas 2:19. [2] Rom 4:18–21; 5:1; 10:10; Heb 4:16. [3] Gal 2:20. [4] Rom 1:17; Heb 10:10. [5] Rom 3:20–26; Gal 2:16; Eph 2:8–10. [6] Acts 16:14; Rom 1:16; 10:17; 1 Cor 1:21.

38. Williamson, *Heidelberg Catechism*, 38.

for me.[39] A person with true faith, comments Kevin DeYoung, does not merely believe Jesus died for sinners, but that he died for him or her.[40] This true faith, and thus assurance, is a work of the Holy Spirit in the heart of the redeemed. This working of the Spirit is in conjunction with, and not apart from, the gospel.

In sum, assurance of salvation has an objective basis in God's truthfulness to his promises mediated through the mind, but it also has a personal basis in the work of the Holy Spirit in the heart. Faith and assurance, in the conception of the HC, are not separable. Faith, by definition, entails assurance. Assurance, then, grows out of faith, or to put differently, assurance is essential to faith. To believe is to be assured.

By stating that "this faith the Holy Spirit works in my heart by the gospel," the HC's conception of assurance is Spirit-centric and gospel-centric. This understanding of assurance is in a similar vein to John Calvin's view on faith and assurance:

> Now we shall possess a right definition of faith if we call it a firm and certain knowledge of God's benevolence toward us, founded upon the truth of the freely given promise in Christ, both revealed to our minds and sealed upon our hearts through the Holy Spirit.[41]

A. 21 of the HC, however, does not mention the intensity of saving faith, which directly impacts assurance. Q. 86 obliquely addresses this issue through explicating the relationship between assurance and good works in a believer's life:

Q. 86: Since we have been delivered from our misery by grace alone through Christ, without any merit of our own, why must we yet do good works?

A. 86: Because Christ, having redeemed us by His blood, also renews us by His Holy Spirit to be His image, so that with our whole life we may show ourselves thankful to God for His benefits,[1] and He may be praised by us.[2] Further, that *we ourselves may be assured of our faith by its fruits,*[3] and that by our godly walk of life we may win our neighbors for Christ.[4][42]

---

39. Bruggink, *Guilt, Grace, and Gratitude,* 59.

40. DeYoung, *Good News We Almost Forgot,* 46.

41. Calvin, *Institutes,* 3.2.7 (551).

42. [1] Rom 6:13; 12:1–2; 1 Pet 2:5–10. [2] Matt 5:16; 1 Cor 6:19–20. [3] Matt 7:17–18; Gal 5:22–24; 2 Pet 1:10–11. [4] Matt 5:14–16; Rom 14:17–19; 1 Pet 2:12; 3:1–2.

One component of assurance, as it states here, comes from the fruits in the life of the Christian. A. 86 points to the subjective aspect of assurance. This subjectivity is not based on the feeling of the Christian but the fruits.[43] The strength of the assurance, in other words, is a function of the strength of the fruits. Since believers' fruits vary, their assurance also differs accordingly.

D. ASSURANCE OF SALVATION IN WCF

While assurance is implicit in the definition of faith in the HC, it is explicit in chapter 18 of the WCF entitled "Of the Assurance of Grace and Salvation." There, in four sections, the WCF addresses the validity, basis, fruits, and restoration of assurance.

1. Although hypocrites and other unregenerate men may vainly deceive themselves with false hopes and carnal presumptions of being in the favor of God, and estate of salvation[1] (which hope of theirs shall perish):[2] yet such as truly believe in the Lord Jesus, and love him in sincerity, endeavoring to walk in all good conscience before him, may, in this life, be certainly assured that they are in the state of grace,[3] and may rejoice in the hope of the glory of God, which hope shall never make them ashamed.[4]44

2. This certainty is not a bare conjectural and probable persuasion grounded upon a fallible hope;[5] but an infallible assurance of faith founded upon the divine truth of the promises of salvation,[6] the inward evidence of those graces unto which these promises are made,[7] the testimony of the Spirit of adoption witnessing with our spirits that we are the children of God,[8] which Spirit is the earnest of our inheritance, whereby we are sealed to the day of redemption.[9]45

3. This infallible assurance doth not so belong to the essence of faith, but that a true believer may wait long, and conflict with many difficulties before he be partaker of it:[10] yet, being enabled by the Spirit to know the things which are freely given him of God, he may, without extraordinary revelation, in the right use of ordinary means, attain thereunto.[11] And therefore it is the duty of everyone to give all diligence

43. Clark, *Recovering the Reformed Confession*, 113–15.

44. [1] Job 8:13; Mic 3:11; Deut 29:19; John 8:41. [2] Matt 7:22. [3] 1 John 2:3; 3:14, 18, 19, 21, 24; 5:13. [4] Rom 5:2, 5.

45. [5] Heb 6:11, 19. [6] Heb 6:17–18. [7] 2 Pet 1:4–5, 10–11; 1 John 2:3; 3:14; 2 Cor 1:12. [8] Rom 8:15–16. [9] Eph 1:13–14; 4:30; 2 Cor 1:21–22.

to make his calling and election sure,[12] that thereby his heart may be enlarged in peace and joy in the Holy Ghost, in love and thankfulness to God, and in strength and cheerfulness in the duties of obedience,[13] the proper fruits of this assurance; so far is it from inclining men to looseness.[14]46

4. True believers may have the assurance of their salvation divers ways shaken, diminished, and intermitted; as, by negligence in preserving of it, by falling into some special sin which woundeth the conscience and grieveth the Spirit; by some sudden or vehement temptation, by God's withdrawing the light of his countenance, and suffering even such as fear him to walk in darkness and to have no light:[15] yet are they never utterly destitute of that seed of God, and life of faith, that love of Christ and the brethren, that sincerity of heart, and conscience of duty, out of which, by the operation of the Spirit, this assurance may, in due time, be revived;[16] and by the which, in the meantime, they are supported from utter despair.[17]47

WCF 18.1 addresses the validity of assurance. It clearly states the possibility of a false assurance whereby the unregenerate deceive themselves "with false hopes and carnal presumptions of being in the favor of God," thinking that they possess salvation when they do not.[48] It also asserts that the regenerate, in this life, may be "certainly assured they are in the state of grace." It thus refutes, in no uncertain terms, the teaching of the Roman Church, where assurance is only for the rarest few with direct revelation from God. Here, the WCF delineates true belief in three dimensions: "believe in the Lord Jesus," "love him in sincerity," and "endeavoring to walk in all good conscience before him," which corresponds, respectively, to a Christian's knowing, being, and doing.

Assurance, notes WCF 18.2, is not only possible but infallible because it is "not a bare conjectural and probable persuasion grounded upon a fallible hope." Specifically, it provides the basis of assurance of salvation in several aspects. The "divine truth of the promises of salvation" is an objective basis of salvation founded upon God's words. The "inward evidence

46. [10] 1 John 5:13; Isa 1:10; Mark 9:24 (see also Pss 77; 88). [11] 1 Cor 2:12; 1 John 4:13; Heb 6:11–12; Eph 3:17–19. [12] 2 Pet 1:10. [13] Rom 5:1, 2, 5; 14:17; 15:13; Eph 1:3–4; Ps 4:6–7; 119:32. [14] 1 John 2:1–2; Rom 6:1–2; Titus 2:11, 12, 14; 2 Cor 7:1; Rom 8:1, 12; 1 John 3:2–3; Ps 130:4; 1 John 1:6–7.

47. [15] Song 5:2, 3, 6; Ps 51:8, 12, 14; Eph 4:30–31; Ps 77:1–10; Matt 26:69–72; Ps 31:22 (Ps 88 throughout); Isa 50:10. [16] 1 John 3:9; Luke 22:32; Job 13:15; Ps 73:15; 51:8, 12; Isa 50:10. [17] Mic 7:7–9; Jer 32:40; Isa 54:7–10; Ps 22:1 (Ps 88 throughout).

48. False assurance is a possibility as expounded by Jesus at the end of the Sermon on the Mount (Matt 7:21–23).

of those graces unto which these promises are made" is a subjective basis related to evidence of a changed life. The "testimony of the Spirit of adoption witnessing with our spirits that we are the children of God" is another basis founded on the conviction by the Holy Spirit regarding believers' adoption. This Spirit of adoption is also the Spirit who is "the earnest of our inheritance, whereby we are sealed to the day of redemption." The "earnest" is a deposit or an initial down payment that guarantees the full payment in the future. The Holy Spirit, given as a gift to the believers, is the earnest for ensuring a future inheritance. This eschatological hope of believers, sustained by perseverance, will culminate at glorification.

John Frame correctly identifies the bases of assurance in WCF 18.2 as corresponding, respectively, to the doctrines of justification, sanctification, and adoption.[49] Perseverance and glorification are also implied in WCF 18.2 through the clause "we are sealed to the day of redemption." Perseverance is guaranteed because the Spirit is the "earnest" of believers' inheritance. This perseverance will continue and seal "to the day of redemption," which is the consummation of salvation in glorification when believers will receive their glorified resurrected bodies. Perseverance and glorification constitute the eschatological dimension of the basis of assurance. Hence, based on the language of WCF 18.2, assurance is grounded on justification, sanctification, adoption, perseverance, and glorification, in that order.

Because assurance of salvation has both an objective and a subjective appropriation as delineated in WCF 18.2, so WCF 18.3, dealing with the fruits of this assurance, can deduce that "this infallible assurance doth *not* so belong to the essence of faith." Possessing the assurance of one's salvation, in other words, is not essential to faith.[50] Saving faith, then, does not necessarily produce assurance. A person, therefore, does not have to possess assurance to be in a state of grace.[51]

Indeed, a person may have "true faith, and sufficient true faith to justify him and finally save him, and yet may not have enough of faith or of its fruits to enable him to attain to assurance."[52] This formulation is opposed to the spirit of the HC in which assurance is part and parcel of faith. How does one interpret the disparity between the HC and the WCF regarding the grounds of assurance?

49. Frame, *Systematic Theology*, 1003–7. In addition to sanctification, the "inward evidence of those graces unto which these promises are made" points to fruits of regeneration as well.

50. Sproul, *Truths We Confess*, 235.

51. Sproul, *Truths We Confess*, 236.

52. Whyte, *Exposition on Shorter Catechism*, 128.

"A true believer," states WCF 18.3, "may wait long before he be partaker of it." The Westminster divines thus distinguished between *initial* faith, which "may or may not include full assurance of salvation" and *developed* faith, which "reflects upon itself and reaches assurance of salvation."[53] If assurance were of the essence of faith, comments David Dickson on WCF 18.3, then "there should not be any degrees of faith, which is contrary to Mark 9:14; Matt 8:10; 15:28."[54]

Assurance of salvation, or more technically, *full* assurance of salvation, is thus not automatic and guaranteed of true believers. Christians must diligently make their calling and election sure (2 Pet 1:10) by intentionally cultivating assurance through "the right use of ordinary means." What are these "ordinary means" whereby assurance can be increased and strengthened? The answer is in WCF 14.1 on saving faith:

> The grace of faith, whereby the elect are enabled to believe to the saving of their souls,[1] is the work of the Spirit of Christ in their hearts,[2] and is ordinarily wrought by *the ministry of the Word*,[3] by which also, and by *the administration of the sacraments*, and *prayer*, it is increased and strengthened.[4][55]

The three means of grace mentioned are the word, the sacraments, and prayer. The resultant fruits of assurance, as stated in WCF 18.3, include peace, joy, love, thanksgiving, and obedience.

Obedience, asserts WCF 18.3, is not only the fruit of salvation but, simultaneously, the fruit of assurance. Assurance and obedience, in this way, form a positive iteration cycle in which assurance induces obedience, which, in turn, strengthens assurance. Since obedience is a fruit of both salvation and assurance, WCF 18.3 refutes the errors of antinomianism and the Roman Church. The former maintains that "none ought or can gather any comfort or assurance of salvation from his own works of holiness,"[56] and the latter argues that assurance inclines believers to looseness.

WCF 18.4 teaches that if true believers fail to nurture assurance by negligence in preserving it, falling into some special sin, succumbing to temptation, God's withdrawing of his countenance, and walking in darkness, they can expect assurance to be "shaken, diminished, and intermitted." The loss of assurance, however, does not imply in any way a loss of salvation. Assurance can be restored through the "seed of God," "life of faith," "love of

---

53. Eaton, *No Condemnation*, 19.

54. Dickson, *Truth's Victory over Error*, 113–14.

55. [1] Heb 10:39. [2] 2 Cor 4:13; Eph 1:17–19; 2:8. [3] Rom 10:14, 17. [4] 1 Pet 2:2; Acts 20:32; Rom 4:11; Luke 17:5; Rom 1:16–17.

56. Dickson, *Truth's Victory over Error*, 112.

Christ and the brethren," "sincerity of heart," and "conscience of duty." Since assurance depends on faith, its nature is changeable because a person's faith can vacillate in life. This dynamic nature of assurance reflects the dynamic nature of faith, described in WCF 14.3 on "Saving Faith":

> This faith is different in degrees, weak or strong;[1] may often and many ways assailed, and weakened, but gets the victory:[2] growing up in many to the attainment of a full assurance, through Christ,[3] who is both the author and finisher of our faith.[4]57

This changeable, subjective aspect of faith described above contrasts itself with the objective aspect stated in WCF 14.2, wherein "the principal acts of saving faith are accepting, receiving, and resting upon Christ alone for justification, sanctification, and eternal life, by virtue of the covenant of grace."58 The juxtaposition of WCF 14.2 and 14.3, however, is characteristic of the formulation of WCF in general, which seeks to maintain a delicate balance in theological expressions and positions.

E. ASSURANCE OF SALVATION IN WESTMINSTER SHORTER AND LARGER CATECHISMS

The Westminster Shorter Catechism (WSC) of 1647 and the Westminster Larger Catechism (WLC) of 1648 have pertinent teachings on assurance. The following is WSC Q. and A. 36:

Q. 36: What are the benefits which in this life do accompany or flow from justification, adoption, and sanctification?

A. 36: The benefits which in this life do accompany or flow from justification, adoption, and sanctification, are, *assurance of God's love*, peace of conscience,[1] joy in the Holy Ghost,[2] increase of grace,[3] and *perseverance therein to the end*.[4]59

Here, assurance is a derived benefit flowing from justification, adoption, and sanctification, rather than a direct benefit flowing from a true faith, which is the stance of the HC. To put it otherwise, while assurance is a direct benefit of faith itself in the HC, it is, in the WSC formulation, only a benefit of faith's benefits. Assurance, in other words, is further "distanced" from faith in the Westminster Standards.

---

57. [1] Heb 5:13–14; Rom 4:19–20; Matt 6:30; 8:10. [2] Luke 22:31–32; Eph 6:16; 1 John 5:4–5. [3] Heb 6:11–12; 10:22. [4] Heb 12:2.

58. WCF 14.2 with reference to John 1:12; Acts 16:31; Gal 2:20; Acts 15:11.

59. [1] Rom 5:1–2, 5. [2] Rom 14:17. [3] Prov 4:18. [4] 1 John 5:13; 1 Pet 1:5.

The WLC also has three questions on assurance, from Q. 79 to Q. 81:

Q. 79: May not true believers, by reason of their imperfections, and the many temptations and sins they are overtaken with, fall away from the state of grace?

A. 79: True believers, by reason of the unchangeable love of God,[1] and his decree and covenant to give them perseverance,[2] their inseparable union with Christ,[3] his continual intercession for them,[4] and the Spirit and seed of God abiding in them,[5] can neither totally nor finally fall away from the state of grace,[6] but are kept by the power of God through faith unto salvation.[7]60

Q. 80: Can true believers be infallibly assured that they are in the estate of grace and that they shall persevere therein unto salvation?

A. 80: Such as truly believe in Christ, and endeavor to walk in all good conscience before him,[1] may, without extraordinary revelation, by faith grounded upon the truth of God's promises, and by the Spirit enabling them to discern in themselves those graces to which the promises of life are made,[2] and bearing witness with their spirits that they are the children of God,[3] *be infallibly assured that they are in the estate of grace, and shall persevere therein unto salvation.*[4]61

Q. 81: Are all true believers at all times assured of their present being in the estate of grace, and that they shall be saved?

A. 81: *Assurance of grace and salvation not being of the essence of faith,*[1] true believers may wait long before they obtain it;[2] and, after the enjoyment thereof, may have it weakened and intermitted, through manifold distempers, sins, temptations, and desertions;[3] yet are they never left without such a presence and support of the Spirit of God as keeps them from sinking into utter despair.[4]62

WLC A. 79 affirms the eternal security of believers, which culminates in final salvation. This future salvation is a result of the Trinitarian acts of the Father's love in granting perseverance, Christ's intercession for believers who are in union with him, and the Spirit's abiding with believers. Assurance of the present salvation, states WLC A. 80, is sure ("infallible"), and

---

60. [1] Jer 31:3. [2] 2 Tim 2:19; Heb 13:20–21; 2 Sam 23:5. [3] 1 Cor 1:8–9. [4] Heb 7:25; Luke 22:32. [5] 1 John 3:9; 2:27; [6] Jer 32:40; John 10:28. [7] 1 Pet 1:5.

61. [1] 1 John 2:3. [2] 1 Cor 2:12; 1 John 3:14, 18, 19, 21, 24; 4:13, 18; Heb 6:11–12. [3] Rom 8:16. [4] 1 John 5:13.

62. [1] Eph 1:13. [2] Isa 50:10; Ps 88. [3] Pss 77:1–12; 51:8, 12; 31:22; 22:1. [4] 1 John 3:9; Job 13:15; Ps 73:15, 23; Isa 54:7–10.

this assurance entails a certainty of final salvation due to the perseverance of the saints. WLC A. 81, in the same spirit as WCF 18.3, explicitly states, "Assurance of grace and salvation not being of the essence of faith." Hence, WCF chapter 18 and WLC A. 81 both deny assurance as of faith's essence, whereas WSC A. 36, WLC A. 80, and HC A. 21 affirm assurance as essential to faith. On the surface, while WLC A. 80 and 81 appear to be contradictory, they merely reflect the careful balance of the Westminster documents. Infallible assurance, to put differently, is *achievable* (A. 80) but not always *available* (A. 81).

F. IS ASSURANCE OF THE ESSENCE OF FAITH?

Why did the HC and the WCF arrive at seemingly dichotomous conclusions regarding whether assurance is of the essence of faith? From a historical perspective, the HC, being produced forty-four years after Martin Luther's Ninety-Five Theses,[63] was still at the prime of the Reformation period during which the Reformers reacted forcibly against the false teachings of Rome, one of which was the doctrine of assurance. Assurance, based on the official teaching of the Roman Church, is not attainable in this life apart from a special revelation from God.

During the Council of Trent, on January 13, 1547, under the Decree concerning Justification, on "Chapter IX: Against the Vain Confidence of Heretics," was this plain teaching:

> For as no pious person ought to doubt the mercy of God, the merit of Christ and the virtue and efficacy of the sacraments, so each one, when he considers himself and his own weakness and indisposition, may have fear and apprehension concerning his own grace, since no one can know with the certainty of faith, which cannot be subject to error, that he has obtained the grace of God.[64]

This statement was produced merely sixteen years before the creation of the HC. Rome's teaching, of course, originated from their understanding of salvation as a joint venture between God and man whereby sinners achieve and maintain salvation in part by their good works. It is thus conceivable in the HC's formulation of the doctrine of saving faith, Ursinus and Olevianus emphasized, as a reaction against Roman Catholicism, the

---

63. There is a span of forty-four years from Oct. 1517 (publication of Luther's Ninety-Five Theses) to Jan. 1563 (publication of the HC).

64. Peterson, "Christian Assurance," 10–11.

objective ground of saving faith. As such, assurance is part and parcel of saving faith and, like saving faith, has the objective foundation in God's promises in Christ, instead of depending on human works.

However, why would the WCF, which came some eighty-four years after the HC, distance assurance from faith? Joel Beeke, in his extensive study of the topic of assurance, investigates this question based on the historical context in the interim period between the HC and the WCF. Beeke has identified two schools of thought on this issue. The first school, populated by William Cunningham,[65] believes that after the HC,

> second and third generation of Protestants had begun to take God's grace for granted. Getting saved by faith was no longer the miracle it was in first-generation Protestantism but had become something quite ordinary. This, in turn, promoted dead orthodoxy in which mere assent was given to the truths of Scripture without a believing response from the heart. Against this background, it became essential to distinguish clearly between an assurance of personal grace and a certainty based on mere assent to Bible truths. And it is here that the English Puritans and Dutch Second Reformation divines . . . attempt to fill a gap in the earlier formulation which had not adequately explained the range of Christian experience with respect to doubt. The sequel is chapter 18 of the Westminster Confession of Faith which clearly separates assurance from faith while maintaining its normativity.[66]

Cunningham further contends that the Reformers, struggling against the false teaching of the formidable Roman ecclesiastical system, were given an extra measure of assurance by God to prevail in their Reformation effort. This context caused the Reformers to regard assurance as essential to saving faith.[67] According to Cunningham, the Westminster divines sought to improve upon, not depart from, magisterial Reformers' formulation of assurance in light of the new pastoral context they encountered in the first third of the seventeenth century. The difference between Calvin and his Westminster followers is thus "substantial but not antithetical."[68]

R. T. Kendall is representative of scholars belonging to the second school of thought. He argues for a sharp discontinuity between Calvin and

---

65. Beeke, "Does Assurance Belong," 46n3.

66. Beeke, *Is Assurance of the Essence,* 8.

67. Cunningham, *The Reformers,* 113–14.

68. Beeke, *Quest for Full Assurance,* 17.

his followers on assurance's relationship with faith.[69] His view engendered heated discussions on both sides of the debate.[70] After a thorough study of Calvin and the later Calvinists on the doctrine of assurance, which, in a sense, can approximate the difference between the HC and the WCF on this topic, Beeke concludes:

> The discrepancy between Calvin and Calvinism on faith and assurance was largely quantitative and methodological. In other words, it was a matter of emphasis and method, rather than qualitative or substantial. The present writer has shown elsewhere that these quantitative differences stem largely from a newly evolving emphasis in the pastoral context of the post-Reformation period.... Notwithstanding different emphases on the question of personal assurance of faith, both Calvin and the Calvinists were fundamentally of one mind on assurance.[71]

Nonetheless, regarding Calvin and his British and Dutch followers, scholars do not have a consensus on the question of whether assurance is of the essence of faith.

Can the discrepancy between the HC and the WCF be a matter of semantics and nomenclature? WCF 18.3 says, "*Infallible* assurance doth not so belong to the essence of faith." Did the Westminster divines specifically intend only an "*infallible* assurance" or a "*full* assurance" as not belonging to the essence of faith, whereas the Heidelberg writers intended a "*general* assurance" as belonging to the essence of faith?[72] Such is the viewpoint of Paul Chang, who, citing the usage of the term "full assurance" and "infallible assurance" in WCF, argues that "implicitly the Westminster Divines made a distinction between *full* or *infallible* assurance and assurance *in general.*"[73]

Chang contends that the WCF wedges a distance between assurance and faith out of the pastoral concern to allow "Christians to relieve their afflicted conscience by examining their good works and inward sanctification

---

69. Kendall, *Calvin and English Calvinism.*

70. Joel Beeke identifies twenty-one other scholars sympathetic to Kendall's view; see Beeke, *Assurance of Faith,* 5n3. Critics of Kendall are many, among them Paul Helm, *Calvin and the Calvinists*; Joel Beeke, "Faith and Assurance"; and Richard Muller, *Unaccommodated Calvin,* 6, 17, 64, 159–62, 172.

71. Beeke, "Does Assurance Belong," 48; Beeke, "Faith and Assurance," 49–51.

72. G. I. Williamson comments that "if all true believers are required to have *full* assurance as the essence of saving faith, there would be no need to exhort them because, being believers, they would on this view already have it." Williamson, *Westminster Confession of Faith,* 175.

73. Chang, "John Calvin on Assurance," 126.

so that they can wait to enjoy in due time the testimony of the Holy Spirit."[74] In the opinion of the present writer, Chang's assessment is very plausible.

G. SUMMARY

The HC and the WCF arrive at seemingly different conclusions regarding whether assurance is of the essence of faith. One can understand this discrepancy by distinguishing between a general versus a full assurance. The former is of the essence of faith, and the latter is not. Nevertheless, both the HC and the WCF have not tethered assurance to adoption in such a way that adoption becomes the primary lens from which to comprehend assurance. The exegetical basis of understanding assurance is the subject of Part III of the book.

74. Chang, "John Calvin on Assurance," 132–33.

PART III

Exegetical Analysis

Chapter 5

Assurance in Romans 8:12–17

The New Testament is not silent on the topic of assurance of salvation.[1] We will present in this chapter the view of the apostle Paul on assurance. The critical text or *locus classicus* of the adoption-centric understanding of assurance is Rom 8:12–17. The Epistle to the Romans not only epitomizes the quintessence of Pauline's theological thought, encompassing all significant disciplines of theology, but chapter 8 of Romans, especially, represents the climax of Paul's exposition of what constitutes assurance. Assurance of adoption, as this chapter will demonstrate, is at the heart of Paul's understanding of assurance of salvation.

A. AN EXEGETICAL-THEOLOGICAL STUDY OF ROMANS 8:12–17

The book of Romans divides into four main sections: introduction (1:1–17), doctrinal teaching (1:18—11:36), practical exhortation (12:1—15:13), and personal greetings (15:14—16:17). Within the doctrinal teaching section, 1:18—3:20 addresses the universality of sin and the need for righteousness. The next section, 3:21—8:39, presents God's remedy for sins by providing righteousness through faith in Christ. It entails justification (3:21—5:21),

---

1. The passages pertaining to believers' assurance and confidence include John 10:14–15; Rom 5:5; 8:15–16, 38–39; 2 Cor 1:21–22; 13:5; Eph 1:13–14; 3:16–19; 2 Tim 1:12; Heb 3:6; 4:6, 16; 6:18–19; 10:19–22; 1 John 1:3–4; 2:3–5, 10; 3:14, 17, 19, 24; 5:13, 20.

sanctification (6:1—8:11), and adoption (8:12–39). The last section, 9:1—11:36, deals with God's righteousness vindicated through his relationship with Israel, wherein God remains faithful despite Israel's unfaithfulness. Table 4 shows the structure of the first eight chapters of Romans.

Table 4: The structure of Romans 1 to 8

Doctrine	Romans	Theme
Justification	1:1—3:20	The need of justification
	3:21–31	The means of justification
	4:1–25	The examples of justification
	5:1–11	The blessings of justification
	5:12–21	The basis of justification
Sanctification	6:1–23	Sanctification and Christ
	7:1–25	Sanctification and the Law
	8:1–11	Sanctification and the Spirit
Adoption	8:12–17	Adoption and assurance
	8:18–30	Adoption and bodily redemption, perseverance, glorification
	8:31–39	Adoption and final victory

1. Contextual Analysis of Romans 8:12–17

A contextual analysis of 8:12–17 shows that this passage situates in the coherent unit of chapters 5 to 8.[2] The purpose of 8:12–17 will emerge if one follows Paul's train of thought in these four chapters. After a clear exposition of the imputation of God's righteousness through his act of justification by faith alone (3:21–31), Paul illustrates this justification in the lives of Abraham and David (4:1–25).[3] Paul, in 5:1–11, then states the results of this justification, which are peace with God (5:1–2), joy in tribulation (5:3–8), and salvation from God's wrath (5:9–11). Next, Paul explains that just as

2. In each of the chapters 5 to 8, Jerry McCant observes, the first subsection is a basic statement concerning the life promised for the person who is righteous by faith. Also, the occurrence of similar phrases at the end of the chapters—"in Christ Jesus our Lord," "through Jesus Christ our Lord," and "in Christ Jesus our Lord"—has the effect of binding the chapters together. McCant, "Wesleyan Interpretation," 68.

3. Abraham's righteousness, Paul notes, is not based on works (4:1–8), or circumcision (4:9–12), or the law (4:13–15), but faith in God's promise (4:16–25). In Rom 4:7–8, Paul also quotes David from Ps 32:1–2 in support of his thesis that justification is by faith, not of works.

the guilt of sin universally applies to every human being via the offense of the federal headship of Adam (5:12–14), so likewise justification from sin applies to the elect via the righteousness of the federal headship of Christ (5:15–17). As such, the reign of sin leads to death, but the reign of grace through righteousness leads to eternal life (5:18–21).

Paul ushers in the theme of the impartation of righteousness through God's work of sanctification in chapter 6. This sanctification consists of, first, definitive sanctification (vv. 1–11), which is sometimes called positional sanctification. The two, however, are not identical. Definitive sanctification is based on the historical co-crucifixion of believers' old man with Christ in order that the body of sin might be brought to nothing (Rom 6:6). The power and enslavement of sin are decisively broken once and for all through definitive sanctification. Positional sanctification, in contrast, is based on the consecration of the believers, now having been freed from the enslavement to sin by definitive sanctification, to dedicate themselves to serve their new master, Christ, in holiness.

The second type of sanctification mentioned in chapter 6 is progressive sanctification (vv. 12–23). Whereas the basis of definitive sanctification is the believers' union with Christ in his death and resurrection, the means of progressive sanctification is through believers becoming slaves of righteousness by yielding their bodies to it.

At this point, Paul's readers might have the impression that sanctification is quite straightforward and easy. The Christians merely need to present their bodies to righteousness, and the fruits will be sanctification (6:22). Paul thus interjects the topic of the relationship between the law and sanctification in chapter 7. Sanctification is not that easy after all, Paul shows, due to the interaction between the law and the residual, indwelling sin in believers.

The word "law" (νόμος) is a keyword in chapter 7. It appears two times in chapter 6,[4] four times in chapter 8,[5] but sixteen times in chapter 7.[6] The main idea of this chapter is the believers' relationship with the law. Though the law has released the believers (7:1–6), the law is still exploited by sin (7:7–13), resulting in an internal and painful struggle between the law of God and the law of sin (7:14–25). The purpose of 7:14–25 is to illustrate that a Christian cannot be delivered and sanctified by the law. The "I" (ἐγώ) in this passage is Paul himself as a mature Christian.[7] The point is that not even

4. Rom 6:14, 15. The frequency is appearing once per 11.5 verses.

5. Rom 8:2, 3, 4, 7. The frequency is appearing once per 9.8 verses.

6. Rom 7:1, 2, 3, 4, 5, 6, 7, 8, 9, 12, 14, 16, 21, 22, 23, 25. The frequency is appearing once per 1.6 verses.

7. The Greek ἐγώ appears a total of six times in five verses in this pericope (7:14, 17, 20, 24, 25). Scholars have hotly debated the identity of ἐγώ, possibilities include (1) Paul

Paul can achieve sanctification by living out God's law as best as he can, due to the law of sin residing in him that struggles against the law of God (7:23).

Then, in chapter 8, Paul presents the secret of how Christians can be victorious in sanctification—through relying on the Holy Spirit, who is the Spirit of life (8:1–11), the Spirit of adoption (8:12–17), and the Spirit of firstfruits (8:18–30) who will assure believers of the eternal love of God (8:31–39). The dominant motif in this chapter is assurance. Along this line, the chapter divides into four major sections: assurance of life in the Spirit (8:1–11), assurance of adoption (8:12–17), assurance of future glory amid present suffering (8:18–30), and assurance of final victory in God's abiding love in Christ Jesus (8:31–39).

Romans chapter 8 can also rightly be called the "chapter of the Spirit" as there are twenty-one mentions of the various forms of πνεῦμα (spirit), compared with only two in chapters 5 to 7 (5:5 and 7:6).[8] The activities of the Spirit depicted are variegated. The Spirit sets believers free in Christ (v. 1); leads them to live a life of righteousness (vv. 4–5, 14); indwells them (v. 9); imparts life (vv. 10–11); assures believers of their adoption (v. 15); testifies that believers are children of God (v. 16); gives himself to believers as firstfruits (v. 23); helps believers in weakness (v. 26); and intercedes for them in prayer (vv. 26–27).

From the contextual analysis above, 8:12–17 is in the larger realm of sanctification in Romans chapters 6 to 8.[9] Paul is portraying the reality of the sanctification experience as consisting of the totality of these three chapters. Though Christians are already definitively sanctified and are in the process of progressive sanctification (Rom 6), they are still struggling with sin.[10] This inability to eradicate sin in their lives is due to the law of sin residing in believers, which fights against the law of God (Rom 7). Even so, deliverance against and final victory over sin is assured by relying on the Spirit (Rom 8). Alternatively, sanctification necessitates the mortification of sin. In brief, sanctification entails believers' death and resurrection with Christ (Rom 6), recognizing themselves as being dead to the law (Rom 7), and living in the Spirit (Rom 8).

---

as a mature Christian or Paul as a Jew under the law; (2) Paul before his conversion; and (3) the experience of a generic human being who tries to live a moral life based on his own strength. See Hart, "Paul as Weak in Faith," 317–43.

8. The frequency of various forms of πνεῦμα appearing in chapter 8 is once per 1.9 verses, compared with once per 21 verses in chapter 5 and once per 25 verses in chapter 7. There is no occurrence in chapter 6.

9. Edwards, *Romans*, 156.

10. It is well known that "sin" (singular) is personified throughout Romans chapters 5 to 8. There is no occurrence of "sins" (plural) in these four chapters.

Paul commences Rom 8 with a proclamation of the effect of justification: "There is therefore now no condemnation for those who are in Christ Jesus." The reason is given by the γὰρ in v. 2, "For the law of the Spirit of life has set you free in Christ Jesus from the law of sin and death." Then, from vv. 3–11, the unmistakable keywords are "flesh" and the "Spirit," where the various forms of σάρξ and πνεῦμα occur ten times each. The flesh is set directly against the Spirit in four instances (vv. 4, 5, 6, 9). The gist of the matter is that walking (v. 4), living (v. 5), and setting the mind on the flesh (v. 6) instead of the Spirit leads to death, not life. "Anyone who does not have the Spirit of Christ," Paul concludes, "does not belong to him" (v. 9).

The pericope of 8:12-17 thematically serves two functions. On the one hand, it continues the topic of sanctification, which Paul commences in Chapter 6 and, in a broad way, extends to the end of Chapter 8. On the other hand, it decisively introduces a new theme, the adoption of believers into God's family, which dominates the balance of Chapter 8. Sanctification and adoption, like justification and sanctification, are distinct but inseparable. However, it is significant that Paul deals with adoption only after he has expounded on justification and sanctification. Adoption, in other words, does not arise from a vacuum. God's acts of justification and definitive sanctification are the foundation of adoption. God can neither admit people who are still legally guilty before his court of justice into his family nor accept those who are still in bondage to the reign of sin and death as his sons. In this sense, adoption rises above justification and sanctification as the climax of not only salvation but also Romans chapter 8.

2. Text of Romans 8:12–17

C. M. Kempton Hewitt conducted a most extensive study of the history of interpretation of this passage. There, he finds no textual criticism issue in the pericope.[11] This section, as such, begins with the pericope in Greek in its basic structure, alongside the present author's literal English translation, in Table 5.[12]

---

11. In his 727-page doctrinal dissertation, he systematically covers six periods of interpretation: Greek patristic period, Latin patristic period, the Middle Ages, the Reformation age, the post-Reformation period, and the modern era. Hewitt, *Life in the Spirit*, 7.

12. In the translation, the words in italics are absent in the original Greek but are added here for clarification. Furthermore, to highlight the continuous nature of the action, all present active indicative verbs are translated using the English present continuous tense instead of the simple present tense.

Table 5: The Greek text of Romans 8:12–17 and its English translation

Verse	Greek Text of Romans 8:12–17	English Translation of Romans 8:12–17
12	Ἄρα οὖν, ἀδελφοί, ὀφειλέται ἐσμὲν οὐ τῇ σαρκὶ τοῦ κατὰ σάρκα ζῆν,	So then, brothers, we are debtors, not *to* the flesh, to live according to the flesh,[13]
13	εἰ γὰρ κατὰ σάρκα ζῆτε, μέλλετε ἀποθνῄσκειν· εἰ δὲ πνεύματι τὰς πράξεις τοῦ σώματος θανατοῦτε, ζήσεσθε.	for if you are living[14] according to *the* flesh, you are about to die,[15] but if *by the* Spirit you are putting to death the deeds of the body, you will live.
14	ὅσοι γὰρ πνεύματι θεοῦ ἄγονται, οὗτοι υἱοὶ θεοῦ εἰσιν.	For all being led by *the* Spirit of God, these[16] are sons of God.
15	οὐ γὰρ ἐλάβετε πνεῦμα δουλείας πάλιν εἰς φόβον ἀλλὰ ἐλάβετε πνεῦμα υἱοθεσίας ἐν ᾧ κράζομεν· αββα ὁ πατήρ.	For you did not receive a spirit[17] of slavery again into fear, but you received Spirit of adoption in whom[18] we are crying out, "Abba! Father!"
16	αὐτὸ τὸ πνεῦμα συμμαρτυρεῖ τῷ πνεύματι ἡμῶν ὅτι ἐσμὲν τέκνα θεοῦ.	The Spirit himself is testifying with/to[19] our spirit that we are children of God.
17	εἰ δὲ τέκνα, καὶ κληρονόμοι· κληρονόμοι μὲν θεοῦ, συγκληρονόμοι δὲ Χριστοῦ, εἴπερ συμπάσχομεν ἵνα καὶ συνδοξασθῶμεν.	And if children, then heirs, heirs indeed of God, and fellow heirs with Christ, if indeed we are suffering *with him* so that we might be glorified *with him*.

13. For a literal translation, the second half of the verse should be translated as "to live according to the flesh" because the word "flesh" appears twice in the verse. NIV translates it as "to live according to it."

14. ζῆτε is second person plural present active indicative, so it is better translated as "you are living," not "you live." The phrase "you are living" is contrasted with "you are putting to death" (θανατοῦτε) in the second half of the verse.

15. ἀποθνῄσκειν is a present active infinitive, so it should be translated as "to die" instead of "will die" or "must die."

16. The demonstrative nominative masculine pronoun οὗτοι (these) is not translated in ESV, NIV, and RSV but is correctly translated as "these" in NASB.

17. It should be translated "a spirit" instead of "the spirit" because the Greek does not have a definite article.

18. ἐν ᾧ is translated as "in whom" instead of "by whom" (ESV), "by him" (NIV), or "by which" (NASB).

19. Whether συμμαρτυρεῖ should be translated as bearing witness "with" or "to" will be discussed in detail later.

3. Exegesis of Romans 8:12–17

A cursory glance at the passage reveals its embodying of many critical theological concepts: the antithesis between the flesh (σάρξ) and the Spirit (πνεῦμα) (v. 12–13); the leading of the Spirit and sonship (v. 14); adoption and prayer (v. 15); assurance, the witnessing of the Spirit, Pauline anthropology (v. 16); and heirship, suffering, and glorification (v. 17).

Despite the richness of theological thoughts contained therein, this passage is a coherent unit consisting of two parts. The first, vv. 12–13, speaks of the obligation of believers to mortify the flesh. The second, vv. 14–17, addresses the power needed to perform that mortification, which is enabled by the Spirit in his ministry of assurance. The Spirit assures believers they are adopted sons of God, thereby supplying the necessary power and confidence to put to death the deeds of the body. Verses 14–17 form the central tenet of this periscope, which manifests a sandwich structure: with the top (vv. 14–15) and bottom (v. 17) layers being adoption, while the central meat is believers' assurance (v. 16).

The passage also exhibits an A–B–A'–B' structure where A is vv. 12–13 with A' v. 15; and B is v. 14 with B' vv. 16–17. The contrast between the flesh and the Spirit in vv. 12–13 parallels that between the spirit of slavery and the Spirit of adoption in v. 15. Similarly, the respective consequence of death and life by following the flesh and Spirit in vv. 12–13 parallels the fear and "Abba! Father!" in v. 15. Also, the twin themes of the Spirit of God and sons of God in v. 14 repeat in v. 16, where "sons of God" in v. 14 echoes the "children of God" in v. 16. This parallelism is followed by v. 17 with an explanation of what "children of God" entails, namely, heirship, suffering, and glory. The following is a more detailed exegesis of the passage.

V. 12. Verses 12–13 serve both as the conclusion of the previous section of "life in the Spirit" (vv. 1–11) and the introduction of the next section of "the Spirit of adoption" (vv. 14–17). There is a shift in focus, clearly, from the proclamation of what God has done for believers in Christ through his Spirit (vv. 1–11) to the exhortation of how they ought to live (vv. 12–13).

Verse 12 starts with two specific identifiers, Ἄρα οὖν (so then) and ἀδελφοί (brothers), signaling that vv. 12–17 are the beginning of a new section. Ἄρα οὖν is an exclusively Pauline expression that appears eleven times in his epistles, seven of which are from Romans. In each instance, it signals the commencement of a new conclusion based on a previous discussion or argument.[20] The immediate context preceding Ἄρα οὖν is Rom 8:1–11, the summary being Christians walk not according to the flesh but the Spirit who

---

20. It appears in Rom 5:18; 7:3, 25; 8:12; 9:16; 9:18; 14:12, 19.

indwells them. Immediately following Ἄρα οὖν is the addressee ἀδελφοί (brothers), which, when used at the beginning of a sentence in Romans, always denotes a new emphasis.[21]

The clear message of this new section is: "We are debtors, not to the flesh, to live according to the flesh." This message is not new, but a conclusion based upon the argument developed in vv. 1–11. The gist of the argument is in v. 6, "For to set the mind on the flesh [σαρκὸς] is death, but to set the mind on the Spirit is life and peace." Since following after the flesh is death, believers are not debtors to the flesh to live according to it. The exhortation not to live according to the flesh is a poignant reminder that neither regeneration nor adoption can eradicate the flesh. Its presence is real (7:14, 18, 23). The only way to face it, as instructed in v. 13b, is to mortify it.

V. 13. After stating the positional truth in v. 12 that Christians are not debtors to the flesh to live according to it, Paul employs a tight, persuasive logic that propels the argument from v. 13 to v. 15 via three consecutive instances of γάρ (for, since). The first γάρ, at the beginning of v. 13, gives the reason for the conclusion stated in v. 12. It explains why Christians are not debtors to the flesh by laying out the dichotomous consequences of living according to the flesh versus the Spirit. The choice between the two kinds of living is a matter of life and death. If believers are living according to the flesh as a continuous lifestyle,[22] they will die.[23] If their lifestyle characterizes putting to death[24] the deeds of the body,[25] they will live.

The Greek word translated as "deeds" is πράξεις, which means "evil or disgraceful deeds."[26] These deeds of the body are the result of living according to the flesh. The message of 8:13 is an echo of 8:6, 6:11–14, and 6:21–22. Significantly, putting to death the deeds of the body is the responsibility of believers because the subject of θανατοῦτε is second person plural. The strength of mortifying the deeds of the body, however, comes from the Spirit.

21. See Rom 1:13; 7:1, 4; 8:12; 10:1; 11:25; 12:1; 15:14, 30; 16:17.

22. The verb ζῆτε (living) is present active indicative denoting a continuous pattern of living in the flesh as a lifestyle.

23. The dying in view is spiritual death because even those who live according to the Spirit will also die physically. The clause "if you live according to the flesh," Catholic theologian Fitzmyer aptly observes, suggests that "it is still possible for even justified Christians to conduct themselves as self-oriented and flesh-guided individuals." Fitzmyer, *Romans*, 492.

24. The verb θανατοῦτε (putting to death) is present active indicative, signaling this putting to death is a way of life.

25. The body here is σῶμα, but its meaning is like σάρξ, as in the previous verse. James Dunn comments that this is the most negative use of σῶμα in Paul. Dunn, *Romans 1–8*, 449.

26. "πρᾶξις," BDAG, 860.

V. 14. This second γὰρ connects v. 14 with vv. 12–13. The sons of God, it states, are led by the Spirit to live according to the Spirit. The verb ἄγονται (being led) has the rudimentary form of ἄγω. It possesses a wide range of meanings. In the context here, it means to "lead/guide morally or spiritually, lead, encourage."[27] Who are those the Spirit of God is leading? They are those who in vv. 12–13 are living according to the Spirit and putting to death the deeds of the body. The closest parallel in meaning to v. 14 is Gal 5:18 where Paul says, "But if you are led (ἄγεσθε) by the Spirit, you are not under the law." This verse is in the broader section of Gal 5:16–18, which likens to the struggles between the flesh and the Spirit portrayed in Rom 7:14–25 and 8:5–7.

The second part of the verse declares who the sons of God are. They are those who follow the leading of the Spirit of God. In this way, the verse connects the Spirit of God with the sons of God. There is a direct relationship, then, between living according to the Spirit and sonship. The former is the confirmation of the latter.

V. 15. This third γὰρ connects v. 15 with v. 14 by further delineating the characteristics of the sons of God. Who are the sons of God? They are those who "did not receive a spirit of slavery" but the "Spirit of adoption." Three dominant views exist among scholars regarding the meaning of the "Spirit of adoption":[28] the Spirit as the agent of adoption who effects it;[29] the Spirit who anticipates adoption;[30] and the Spirit who expresses adoption by testifying to it.[31] Because of the phrase "to fall *back* into fear" (πάλιν εἰς φόβον), the spirit of slavery (πνεῦμα δουλείας), in the context of this pericope, is the spirit the believers had in their previous state when they were enslaved to the flesh to do the things according to the flesh (v. 12–13).[32]

---

27. Its meaning ranges from "to direct the movement of an object from one position to another; to take into custody, lead away, arrest, legal; to make use of time for a specific purpose, spend, observe; to move away from a position, go." "ἄγω," BDAG, 16–17.

28. Burke, *Message of Sonship*, 147–48. For more recent research on situating the term "Spirit of adoption" in the Roman imperial context, see Lewis, *Paul's "Spirit of Adoption."* The adoption metaphor, Lewis concludes, seeks to assure Paul's gentile readers that their status as children of God is legitimate through adoption. This conclusion is based on the political, social, and religious context of the Roman Empire and Paul's Jewish heritage, Hellenistic upbringing, and Roman citizenship. For understanding "Spirit of adoption" based on the latest research on metaphor theories, see Heim, *Adoption in Galatians and Romans*.

29. The genitive is taken as a predicate in this case. Fee, *God's Empowering Presence*, 566.

30. Adoption is viewed as an eschatological event (Rom 8:23). Barrett, *Romans*, 153.

31. This is undoubtedly true in light of Rom 8:16. Murray, *Romans*, 295.

32. As Leon Morris points out, "Christ had freed them from their bondage to sin;

The word δουλείας comes from δοῦλος, a male slave, which is the common term Paul uses to describe his relationship with Christ, namely, δοῦλος Χριστοῦ Ἰησοῦ (a slave of Christ Jesus, Rom 1:1). This fear, in the social context, is what a slave would have had under a harsh master.[33] In the spiritual realm, it most likely refers to the fear of sin's consequence or even death, as in Heb 2:15.[34] In contrast to the spirit of slavery believers had before their adoption into God's family, believers are now crying out, "Abba! Father!" (αββα ὁ πατήρ), because of the Spirit of adoption (πνεῦμα υἱοθεσίας).[35]

The "Spirit of adoption" has in view the Spirit who "brought about adoption," uniting sinners to Christ through Spirit-wrought faith, thus enabling them to share in Christ's sonship.[36] Jesus himself uttered the peculiar phrase, "Abba, Father," at a moment of great spiritual need, in the garden of Gethsemane (Mark 14:36). The act of calling God their "Abba! Father!" bespeaks both the intimate relationship Christians now enjoy with their Heavenly Father and the obligations they have in ethical living befitting that relationship. "The whole of Christian obedience," comments Cranfield, "is included in this calling God 'Father.'"[37]

This crying did not just happen at conversion, as the present active indicative form of κράζομεν reveals. Instead, it is happening throughout the life of the believer. Paul, therefore, contrasts not only the spirit of slavery with the Spirit of adoption but also the respective consequence of being indwelled by them. The former leads to fear; the latter results in crying out, without fear, "Abba! Father!" This crying out, of course, is a form of prayer.[38]

V. 16. This verse, which is the meat of assurance of adoption, begins with no connecting word, signifying its organic oneness with v. 15. The subject of the verse is the Spirit (τὸ πνεῦμα) and the αὐτὸ preceding it underlines the fact that it is the Spirit *himself* who is testifying. The verb

they must not think that the Spirit would lead them back to it." Morris, *Romans*, 314. Douglas Moo, however, simply views "the spirit of slavery" as a rhetorical device: "The Spirit of God we have received is not a spirit of fear but the Spirit who makes us God's sons." Moo, *Romans*, 261.

33. Kruse, *Romans*, 337.

34. Harrison, "Romans," 92.

35. "Abba" is the Greek transliteration of the Aramaic word for "father." Fitzmyer, *Romans*, 498.

36. Cranfield, *Romans*, 397.

37. Cranfield, *Romans*, 393. Cranfield notes, furthermore, that the crying out, κράζομεν, is used "again and again in the LXX of urgent prayer, being so used in Psalms alone more than forty times." Cranfield, *Romans*, 399.

38. This distinctive cry, Dunn suggests, may bear the imprint of frequent repetition in the devotion of worship. Dunn, *Romans 1–8*, 453.

συμμαρτυρεῖ means to "testify with/to" or "testify."[39] This testifying is a present continuous action due to the present active indicative tense of the verb. This verb appears two other times, in Rom 2:15 and 9:1, both of which speak of the conscience as the subject of testifying.

Scholars hotly debated whether συμμαρτυρεῖ carries the sense of testifying "with" or "to" our spirit (πνεύματι ἡμῶν). It denotes a dual witness in the former case and a single witness in the latter. The content of the witness is, "we are children of God" (ἐσμὲν τέκνα θεοῦ). Hence, v. 15 and v. 16 complement each other. The former accentuates, "God is our Father," and the latter, "we are God's children."

V. 17. This verse starts with εἰ δὲ τέκνα, which acts as a connecting phrase that ties it closely with v. 16. Adoption is an immensely eschatological divine action because it imparts sonship, which guarantees eschatological heirship. The meaning of the word "heirs" (κληρονόμοι) is to "give title to a possession."[40] Amazingly, the inheritance is not some material possession, not even some spiritual blessings, but God himself (κληρονόμοι μὲν θεοῦ).[41] Believers are heirs indeed of God (κληρονόμοι μὲν θεοῦ)[42] and fellow heirs with Christ (συγκληρονόμοι δὲ Χριστοῦ). As fellow heirs with Christ, believers share the inheritance God gives to Christ.[43]

The evidence of this heirship, ironic to some but comforting to others, is the present suffering with Christ. The ἵνα suggests that the current, continuous suffering is a prerequisite of the future glorification. Putting it otherwise, the privilege of adoption, namely future inheritance, is dispensed along with the responsibility of adoption, the present suffering.[44]

---

39. "συμμαρτυρέω," BDAG, 957.

40. Heirship implies a status in society based on descent from a father in a household. Fitzmyer, *Romans*, 502.

41. Dunn connects this inheritance with Jews' self-understanding that Israel was the Lord's inheritance (Deut 32:9). He comments: "Integral to that national faith was the conviction that God had given Israel the inheritance of Palestine, the promised land. It is this axiom which Paul evokes and refers to the new Christian movement as a whole. . . . Israel's special relationship with God has been extended to all in Christ. And the promise of the land has been transformed into the promise of the kingdom." Dunn, *Romans 1–8*, 462.

42. In the parallel verse in Gal 4:7, it is "heir through God" (κληρονόμος διὰ θεοῦ) instead of "heir of God" (κληρονόμοι μὲν θεοῦ).

43. Kruse, *Romans*, 340.

44. Verse 17 serves as an introduction to the more extended treatment of hope amidst suffering in vv. 18–30.

B. AN EXEGETICAL-THEOLOGICAL
ANALYSIS OF ROMANS 8:12–17

The exegesis of Rom 8:12–17 opens the way for a deeper theological understanding of assurance of adoption. To this end, it is beneficial to posit the following questions through which the exegesis will provide the answer.

1. Who Is Giving the Testimony?

Because συμμαρτυρεῖ is in the present tense, the question is, "who is giving the testimony?" not "who gave the testimony?" Is it a joint witness (God's Spirit witnesses *with* our spirit) or a single witness (God's Spirit witnesses *to* our spirit)? In the former, the Greek τῷ πνεύματι would denote a dative of association (*with* our spirit), whereas the latter would indicate a dative of an indirect object (*to* our spirit).[45]

The majority of modern Bible translations and biblical scholars favor the joint-witness view,[46] while some other scholars and older commentators support the single-witness view.[47] The crux of the interpretation is whether the meaning of συμμαρτυρεῖ is testifying *with* or *to*.[48] Both sides have strengths and weaknesses. The joint-witness view, as will be demonstrated, has more substantial merits with fewer interpretive issues.

Old Testament law, those who favor the joint-witness view note, requires at least two to three witnesses to execute a death penalty (Deut 17:6) or establish a criminal charge (Deut 19:15).[49] More importantly, the New Testament confirms this principle in the case of church discipline (Matt 18:16), charges against a believer (2 Cor 13:1), and accusations against an

---

45. Wallace, *Greek Grammar*, 160.

46. For an extended list of Bible translations and modern scholars who support the joint-witness view, see footnote 11 of Gundersen, "Adoption, Assurance," 33. The Bible translations include KJV, NKJV, ASV, NASB, RSV, NRSV, ESV, HCSB, NIV, TNIV, JB, NJB, and Moffatt. The scholars include Thomas R. Schreiner, Douglas J. Moo, James D. G. Dunn, John Murray, Charles Hodge, William G. T. Shedd, William Sanday, Arthur C. Headlam, R. C. H. Lenski, William Hendriksen, Robert Jewett, William Barclay, Sinclair B. Ferguson, and Louis Berkhof.

47. See footnote 12 of Gundersen, "Adoption, Assurance," 33. Translations supporting the single-witness view include Vulgate, Luther's Bible, NET Bible, and NLT. The scholars listed include C. E. B. Cranfield, Daniel B. Wallace, John Calvin, Franz J. Leenhardt, F. Godet, Ernst Käsemann, Leon Morris, and Théo Preiss.

48. Robert Mounce takes a "both-and" approach: "There is no particular reason why the Holy Spirit cannot both witness *to* the regenerated human spirit and consequently *with* it." Mounce, *Romans*, 183.

49. See, for instance, Dunn, *Romans 1–8*, 454.

elder (1 Tim 5:19). The Holy Spirit and the human spirit, therefore, would satisfy this dual-witness requirement to establish a person as a child of God.[50]

The Holy Spirit alone is sufficient, argue opponents of the joint-witness view, as one cannot find a more truthful or reliable witness than God himself. Cranfield famously asks the rhetorical question: "What standing has our spirit in this matter? Of itself, it surely has no right at all to testify to our being sons of God."[51] Daniel Wallace, for instance, argues:

> To see Deut 19:15 as part of the background of this verse is unnecessary. It seems to presuppose that the Spirit's testimony is not good enough if offered by itself. This also presupposes that our testimony, in combination with the Spirit's, is good enough! But elsewhere in the NT a single testimony is often acceptable, especially one offered by God.[52]

Cranfield and Wallace, however, fail to reckon with two critical passages that would significantly undermine their arguments. In John 8:17–18, Jesus says, "In your Law, it is written that the testimony of two people is true. I am the one who bears witness [μαρτυρῶν] about myself, and the Father who sent me bears witness [μαρτυρεῖ] about me." Jesus here recognizes the validity of applying the Mosaic Law of Deut 19:15 even to himself. No one can deny Jesus' testimony is the gold standard of trustworthiness. Still, the Father *also* bears witness about him. In 1 John 5:6–8, the apostle John asserts: "This is he who came by water and blood—Jesus Christ; not by the water only but by the water and the blood. And the Spirit is the one who testifies [μαρτυροῦν] because the Spirit is the truth. For there are three that testify [μαρτυροῦντες]: the Spirit and the water and the blood; and these three agree." Here, even though the Spirit is the one who testifies—and one can hardly argue that his testimony needs further support—the water and the blood still testify.

Significantly, in Rom 8:16, it is the Spirit himself who testifies with our spirit, not our spirit testifies with the Spirit. The issue here, therefore, is not that the Spirit needs believers' testimony, but believers need his. It is

---

50. Trevor Burke makes the point that the dual-witness view is consistent with the Roman practice of adoption in which "the *manicipatio* was carried out in the presence of witnesses, to ensure that the legality of the adoption could be established beyond doubt by one or more of the witnesses." Burke, *Adopted into God's Family*, 150.

51. Cranfield, *Romans*, 403.

52. Wallace, "Witness of the Spirit." He goes on to list Acts 13:22; 15:8; Rom 10:2; Col 4:13; 1 Tim 6:13; Heb 10:15; 11:4; 1 John 5:9–10; and Rev 1:2 as examples of the sufficiency of the singularity of God's witness. These examples, in the opinion of the present writer, do not sufficiently demonstrate that the principle of two to three witnesses established in the OT and NT has been abrogated.

precisely because, in response to Cranfield, a believer's testimony has such a small and feeble standing before God, a much weaker testimony compared with the powerful testimony of the Spirit, that the latter testimony is all the more necessary.[53] The problem is not that the divine testimony is inadequate, which necessitates bolstering from the human testimony, but the reverse.

The word συμμαρτυρέω itself is a compound word consisting of μαρτυρέω (to testify) and the prefix συν- (with). Hence, the natural meaning of the word, on face value, is "to testify with." Moreover, there is a high concentration of συν-prefixed words in the vicinity of Rom 8:16, most of them bearing an associative sense.[54] In particular, there are three συν-prefixed words in v. 17 alone, all having a "together with" meaning.[55]

This unusual linguistic pattern is hard to ignore, lending credence to συμμαρτυρέω as referring to dual witnesses.[56] Besides, the only two other occurrences of συμμαρτυρέω in Romans indicate two witnesses. In 2:15, the gentiles and their conscience testify that the work of the law is written in people's hearts. In 9:1, Paul and his conscience bear witness to his truthfulness. In short, these lexical-linguistic considerations support the dual-witness meaning in 8:16.

If one compares the parallel passage of Gal 4:6 with Rom 8:15, the Holy Spirit and the human spirit are both testifying to believers' adoption as sons. Specifically, in Gal 4:6, it is the Spirit of his Son who is crying, "Abba, Father," testifying, objectively and personally, to believers' status as sons. In Rom 8:15, it is the believers, by the power of the Spirit of adoption, who are crying, "Abba, Father," also testifying, though subjectively, to the same reality. In this way, the Spirit's crying (Gal 4:6) testifies *with* (συμμαρτυρεῖ) believers' crying (Rom 8:15) that they are children of God (8:16) as both are crying, "Abba! Father!" As Ferguson puts it, "There is one cry, but that cry has two sources: the consciousness of the believer and the ministry of the Spirit. Thus, the Spirit bears witness along with believers' spirits that they are God's children in the cry that comes from their lips, 'Abba, Father.'"[57]

---

53. This is the point of 1 John 5:9: "If we receive the testimony of men, the testimony of God is greater." Believers thus need the greater testimony of God.

54. Gundersen, "Adoption, Assurance," 22. He lists nine such συν-prefixed words: συμμαρτυρεῖ (8:16); συγκληρονόμοι, συμπάσχομεν, συνδοξασθῶμεν (8:17); συστενάζει, συνωδίνει (8:22); συνεργεῖ (8:28); συμμόρφους (8:29); συμμαρτυρούσης (9:1).

55. συγκληρονόμοι (joint-heir with), συμπάσχομεν (suffer with), συνδοξασθῶμεν (be glorified with).

56. Such is the view of Ferguson, *Holy Spirit*, 185.

57. Ferguson, *Holy Spirit*, 185. Ferguson, regarding Gal 4:6 and Rom 8:15, argues

2. What Is the Content of the Testimony?

Rom 8:16 explicitly states the content of the testimony, "we are children of God" (ἐσμὲν τέκνα θεοῦ). This testimony imparts assurance of adoption, which is, for all theological and practical purposes, the assurance of salvation. After all, Paul says earlier in 8:9, "Anyone who does not have the Spirit of Christ does not belong to him." However, for those who have the Spirit, the Spirit of adoption, their instinctive cry is "Abba! Father!" In Romans 8, the Spirit does not testify about believers' regeneration, justification, sanctification, or glorification, but their adoption. Therefore, the Spirit in 8:15 is not called the Spirit of regeneration, justification, sanctification, or glorification, but the Spirit of adoption.

The change from "sons of God" (υἱοὶ θεοῦ) in v. 14 to "children of God" (τέκνα θεοῦ) in v. 16 does not hold significance in terms of gender, as the latter merely denotes what the former connotes, that is, the inclusivity of the sexes.[58] Nevertheless, the word "children" appears to highlight the intimate familial relationship, whereas "sons" the legal standing.[59]

3. Who Is Receiving the Testimony?

The primary interpretive conundrum of the joint-witness view is the identity of the recipient of the joint witness. For the single-witness view in which the Spirit testifies *to* our spirit, our spirit is the recipient. When the Spirit testifies *with* our spirit, however, who receives that testimony? God cannot be the recipient because he is omniscient. It is God himself who "predestined us for adoption as sons through Jesus Christ, according to the purpose of his will" (Eph 1:5).

Since the testimony is *"we are* children of God," where the pronoun is the first-person plural, it follows that the recipients of the testimony are all of God's children, including the apostle Paul.[60] Nonetheless, critics of the

---

that "these two statements are best harmonized by recognizing that the cry 'Abba! Father!' is seen by Paul as expressing the coordinated witness of the believer and the Spirit."

58. Garner makes the excellent point that the phrase "sons of God" does not exclude females any more than the term "the bride of Christ" excludes males. Garner, *Sons in the Son*, 53.

59. Harrison, "Romans," 93.

60. If the testimony is *"you are* children of God," one can argue that the Roman Christians need that kind of assurance. If the testimony is *"they are* children of God," one can say that a specific subset of the Christians needs that testimony.

joint-witness view rightly point out the logical issue of this interpretation. Daniel Wallace asks pointedly:

> If "our spirit" refers to our "inner person," as almost all commentators take it, then what is the difference between "our spirit" and "ourselves"? If there is no real difference, what does it mean that "the Spirit bears witness with our spirit to ourselves"? Does this mean that we witness to us? This sounds as if the responsibility to convince myself of my salvation is myself. This interpretation, of course, is refuted on its face.[61]

In response, the joint witness of the Spirit and our spirit is testifying to both an objective and a personal truth, namely, "we are children of God." It is a joint testimony to impart assurance of adoption. As in an earthly case of adoption, there is no logical or judicial fallacy for an adopted child to testify, "I am his adopted son, and he is my adoptive father." That testimony in itself, however, does not carry sufficient weight because there is not a second witness to corroborate it.[62] The much weightier testimony—"he is my adopted son and I am his adoptive father"—would need to come from the adoptive father who initiates and carries out the adoption. This decisive testimony is precisely the import of Rom 8:15–16.

The absence of a conjunction between the two verses (asyndeton) reflects the inherent unity between them. In v. 15, after receiving the Spirit of adoption as sons, the children are crying out, "Abba, Father," in the sense of "God is my adoptive father." In v. 16, the Spirit, in the position of the adoptive father, testifies with the human spirit that "we are children of God"—that is, "we are his adopted children." The fact that the testimony is not "*they* are children of God" indicates that this testimony is not for a third party, but the adopted sons themselves.

4. Why Is the Testimony Needed?

It is one thing if a person is objectively saved by union with Christ through Spirit-created faith; it is quite another if this person has a subjective assurance of this fact. This personal conviction comes from the Spirit's ministry of assurance. The purpose of the testimony is to provide a subjective, personal assurance of adoption, which is equivalent to, for all purposes,

---

61. Wallace, "Witness of the Spirit."

62. This is the objection of the Pharisees in John 8:13 that Jesus is bearing witness to himself, and his testimony is not valid. In response, Jesus says, "Even if I do bear witness about myself, my testimony is true" (John 8:14).

assurance of salvation. This personal appropriation of salvation is a mark of true faith.[63] A person with true faith, Kevin DeYoung correctly points out, does not merely believe Jesus died for sinners, but he died for him or her individually.[64]

The Spirit's testimony is critical because believers' assurance of their adoption is frail at times. Doubts concerning their salvation could arise from within, especially during those moments when they "live according to the flesh" (v. 13). The Spirit's confirmation with the human spirit provides the much-needed assurance that "God is ours" (v. 15) and "we are his" (v. 16). Of importance is the sequence of this reciprocal truth. Stated another way, it is only when God first becomes the Father of believers that believers can be called the children of God, not the other way around.

Attacks on the assurance of salvation could also originate from external sources in the form of accusations. By scrutinizing the context after Rom 8:12–17, there is a series of rapid-fire questions in which Paul asks: If God is for us, who can be against us (v. 31)? Who shall bring any charge against God's elect (v. 33)? Who is to condemn (v. 34)? Who shall separate us from the love of Christ (v. 35)?

What is the antecedent of "who" in Paul's questions? Based on the adversary and accusatory nature of the questions, it is logical and exegetically sensible to conclude that Paul has in mind Satan, whose name means "the Adversary."[65] Satan is also called "the accuser of our brothers . . . who accuses them day and night before our God" (Rev 12:10). It is during these times of spiritual onslaught from the evil one that the Spirit would step in, as a star witness, to testify, along with believers' spirit, that "we are children of God" (v. 16).

5. How Is the Testimony Being Transmitted?

This question is equivalent to "How does the Spirit testify with our spirit"? From a temporal perspective, the testifying of the Spirit is continuous and

---

63. As discussed in Q. 21 of the HC on "What is true faith?" The answer is, "True faith is a sure knowledge whereby I accept as true all that God has revealed to us in His Word. At the same time it is a firm confidence that not only to others, *but also to me*, God has granted forgiveness of sins, everlasting righteousness, and salvation, out of mere grace, only for the sake of Christ's merits. This faith the Holy Spirit works in my heart by the gospel" (italics mine).

64. DeYoung, *Good News We Almost Forgot*, 46.

65. Satan is the transliteration of the Aramaic שָׂטְנָא, meaning, "the Adversary," and is the equivalent of διάβολος (the standard LXX translation). Hagner, *Matthew 1–13*, 68.

active, due to the present tense of the verb συμμαρτυρεῖ. It is not a one-time testimony that happened only at the initial moment of conversion. It is instead an ongoing testimony throughout the lifetime of the believers, from regeneration to glorification, bolstering their assurance of adoption.

This continuous testimony of the Spirit, paradoxically, coexists with the moments of doubt of believers. It is because believers may momentarily choose to walk according to the flesh, which would erode their assurance. When they repent and cry out to God for mercy in their distress, however, the Spirit will once again testify, with their spirits, that they are children of God.

This ongoing testimony, based on v. 16 and its context, is an immediate testimony—without the medium of the word through the mind.[66] Verse 16 says, "The Spirit himself testifies with our spirit that we are children of God." There is no mention of God's words or quotations from Scripture in the vicinity of v. 16.[67] Also, from v. 15, one can deduce that the Spirit's joint testimony with believers' spirit in v.16 is in corroboration of their Spirit-enabled uttering of "Abba! Father!" Hence, the assurance of the Spirit imparts in the context of prayers. The Spirit can certainly prompt believers to recall the words of God as a means of assurance, yet the emphasis here is not the words of God (as in 1 John 5:13), but prayer itself. It is when believers pray and instinctively address God as their "Abba, Father," especially in times of great distress, that their assurance of adoption heightens.[68]

6. How Can Believers Be Sure of Their Adoption?

To put it otherwise, what are the signs believers have obtained assurance of adoption? From Rom 8:12–17, there are several signs. Most importantly, they are not living according to the flesh but by the Spirit, putting down the deeds of the flesh (vv. 12–13). Moreover, they are being led by the Spirit to follow his leading in ethical living (v. 14). Furthermore, they are not in fear but are crying out, instinctively, naturally, and spontaneously, "Abba, Father," in prayers, especially in times of great distress and suffering,[69] just as

66. For a historical perspective in the Puritan tradition regarding how this testimony is transmitted, see Beeke, "Assurance Debate," 276–81.

67. If the Spirit were to testify *to* our spirit instead of *with* our spirit, it would either mean supernatural revelation or testifying through God's words.

68. As Ferguson puts it, "In this very cry for help, the Spirit of God bears witness with our spirits that we are indeed God's children." Ferguson, *Children of the Living God*, 75.

69. An unbeliever, in times of great pain or needs, might also instinctively cry out "God!" or "O God!" but never "Abba! Father!"

Jesus did in the garden of Gethsemane (v. 15).[70] Due to the Spirit's continuous and immediate witnessing with their spirit, they are personally assured they are "children of God" (v. 16). They are experiencing sufferings with Christ but are holding on to the firm hope of future inheritance of God and glorification with Christ (v. 17). If believers are experiencing the above, they will have the assurance of their adoption: God is their Father, and they are God's children. They are assured of their salvation, in other words, through an assurance of their adoption.

C. AN ADOPTION-CENTRIC UNDERSTANDING OF ASSURANCE OF SALVATION

In summary, based on the exegetical-theological analysis of Rom 8:12-17 and the broader context of Romans 8, the translation from slaves to sons, from living according to the flesh to living in obedience to the Spirit, and from fear to crying out, "Abba, Father," entails six aspects. The slaves first need to be redeemed and set free via the payment of a ransom, the very life of God's own Son (v. 32). Second, the freedmen, through the Spirit of adoption, need to be adopted into the family of God as sons (v. 15).[71] The sons, thirdly, through the testifying ministry of the Spirit, need to be assured they are indeed children of the Father (v. 16). Fourth, with the assurance of adoption, the sons are empowered to live a life pleasing to their Father—exhibiting obedient living according to the Spirit (v. 12-13) and being led by the Spirit (v. 14). Fifth, an integral part of this assurance of adoption is that the sons are heirs—heirs of God and fellow-heirs with Christ, which entails and fosters their perseverance in the face of their suffering with Christ (v. 17). Finally, their present suffering is but a prelude to the future glorification with Christ (v. 17). This eschatological glorification is the final installment of believers' adoption, which is the redemption of their bodies (v. 23).[72] These six aspects, in theological terms, signify justification, adoption, assurance, sanctification, perseverance, and glorification, respectively.

70. Dunn comments, "It is precisely because believers found themselves crying to God with the word used by Jesus that they could be so sure that they shared in Jesus' sonship and inheritance (vv. 16–17). The usage is clearly understood as a distinctive badge of Christians." Dunn, *Romans 1–8*, 454.

71. Dunn calls this the crossing of a double gulf in which "the believer's status has been transformed not only from slave to freedman (see on 6:16) but also from freedman to adopted son." Dunn, *Romans 1–8*, 452.

72. The present aspect of adoption in v. 15 and its future aspect in v. 23 once again reveal the tension between "already" and "not yet" in God's children.

D. IS ASSURANCE OF THE ESSENCE OF FAITH?

From the perspective of viewing assurance of adoption as assurance of salvation, the Spirit assures believers they are children of God. There are two sides to this assurance. On the divine side, this assurance is actively, continuously, and immediately imparted by the Spirit to believers, as part of the ministry of assurance of the Spirit. On the human side, believers, especially during the times of prayers in spiritual distress, receive this testimony from the Spirit in conjunction with their spirit that they are children of God.

Therefore, on the one hand, every believer, without exception, will have this assurance of adoption, as Rom 8:14–17 unequivocally teaches. It is in this sense that assurance is of the essence of faith. On the other hand, if assurance means that a believer will always know at every single moment that he or she is a child of God, then the answer is negative. Romans 8:12–13 warns of this exact scenario when believers, in their weakness, choose to live according to the flesh instead of the Spirit. Assurance, in this case, will be severely impaired and undermined, and thus not of the essence of faith.

E. SUMMARY

In the mind of the apostle Paul, assurance of adoption is the essence of assurance of salvation. Assurance is a ministry of the Holy Spirit who personally and immediately testifies with the spirit of believers, in their cry of "Abba, Father," that they are children of God. As children, believers are heirs of God and joint heirs with Christ in his present suffering and future glorification. In the next chapter, we shall see how the apostle John's view of assurance complements that of the apostle Paul.

Chapter 6

Assurance in 1 John

Among the various New Testament letters, the apostle John writes the First Epistle of John with the express purpose of assuring his readers of salvation. This chapter shows that the apostle John holds to a regeneration-centric, sanctification-centric, and perseverance-centric understanding of assurance, which complements the adoption-centric view of the apostle Paul.

A. THE PURPOSE OF 1 JOHN

The apostle John states the purpose of the letter in 5:13, "I write these things to you who believe in the name of the Son of God that you may know that you have eternal life."[1] This statement of purpose implies that true believers may not have, or at least may not attain a sufficient level of, assurance of salvation. The apostle John, therefore, desires to assure his

---

1. Stephen Rockwell argues convincingly that out of thirteen possible candidate verses (1:4; 2:1; 2:7; 2:8; 2:12; 2:13a; 2:13b; 2:14a; 2:14b; 2:14c; 2:21; 2:26; 5:13), 1 John 5:13 is indeed the purpose statement of the entire epistle based on grammatical and structural analysis. Rockwell, "Assurance," 21–26.

readers of this assurance.[2] Assurance, in this respect, is not of the essence of faith, but comes later, as stated in WCF 18.3.[3]

The apostle John wrote the letter to address a crisis caused by the secession of some members influenced by some form of proto-gnosticism.[4] These proto-gnostics were influenced by the early stages of that great, amorphous theosophical hotchpotch that later historians refer to as Gnosticism.[5] One version of this gnostic view claimed that Christ might have "seemed" (Greek *dokeo*; hence, Docetism) to appear in the flesh but did not. To them, the idea Christ would appear "in the flesh" was ridiculous, if not abhorrent.[6] These secessionists left the church, causing the left-behind believers to wonder about their spiritual status. Those who left, the apostle John concluded, were not true believers: "They went out from us, but they were not of us; for if they had been of us, they would have continued with us. But they went out, that it might become plain that they all are not of us" (1 John 2:19).

B. ASSURANCE IN 1 JOHN

A chief emphasis in John's writing is on being born into God's family by the Spirit. At the very outset of the Gospel of John, he states, "But to all who did receive him, who believed in his name, he gave the right to become children of God, who were born, not of blood nor of the will of the flesh nor of the will of man, but of God" (John 1:12–13). Many consider these verses as prooftexts of the doctrine of adoption. Such a view is most likely mistaken because John explicitly states that those who believed in Jesus' name were "born" of God, not adopted by him, with a vast difference between them. The crux of Jesus' conversation with Nicodemus is on being "born again." Jesus told Nicodemus in no uncertain terms, "Unless one is born of water and the Spirit, he cannot enter the kingdom of God" (John 3:5).

While Paul emphasizes adoption as the means to enter God's family, John gives prominence to being born again into God's family. John is the only New Testament writer who calls Christians as "born of God" (ἐκ τοῦ

---

2. The purpose statement of 1 John 5:13 is parallel with and a sequel to the purpose statement of the Gospel of John in John 20:31: "But these are written so that you may believe that Jesus is the Christ, the Son of God, and that by believing you may have life in his name."

3. WCF 18.3: "This infallible assurance doth not so belong to the essence of faith, but that a true believer may wait long, and conflict with many difficulties before he be partaker of it."

4. Carson, "Reflections on Christian Assurance," 27.

5. Carson, "Johannine Perspectives on Assurance," 67.

6. Burge, *Letters of John*, 29.

θεοῦ γεγέννηται, γεγεννημένος ἐκ τοῦ θεοῦ, γεγεννημένον ἐκ τοῦ θεοῦ) or "born of him" (ἐξ αὐτοῦ γεγέννηται).[7] His preferred title for God is "Father,"[8] and his usual expression for believers is "children of God" (τέκνα θεοῦ, τέκνα τοῦ θεοῦ).[9] Being born into God's family is equivalent, in John's mind, to having eternal life. He explicitly states in 5:13 the purpose of his first epistle: "I write these things to you who believe in [πιστεύητε εἰς] the name of the Son of God that you may know that you have eternal life." This eternal life is the life born of water and the Spirit (John 3:5).

John, in other words, adopts a regeneration-centric understanding of assurance based on viewing salvation as the new birth. In light of this understanding, John set forth several "tests" to assure his readers that they did have eternal life. In contrast, it is the secessionists who did not.

C. THE TESTS OF ASSURANCE

Robert Law, in his classic and well-cited treatment of 1 John, demonstrates that there are three cardinal "tests of life"—the test of righteousness, the test of love, and the test of belief—to assess whether a person has eternal life and been born again.

1. The Test of Righteousness

The relevant passages of the test of righteousness include 1:6–10, 2:3–6, 2:15–16, 3:3–10, and 5:2.[10] It is a test of obedience and morality in which believers "walk in the light as He is in the light" (1:7). The first principal passage of this test, stating positively who the children of God are, is 2:3–6:

> 2:3 And by this we know that we have come to know him, if we keep his commandments. 4 Whoever says "I know him" but does not keep his commandments is a liar, and the truth is not in him, 5 but whoever keeps his word, in him truly the love of God is perfected. By this we may know that we are in him: 6 whoever says he abides in him ought to walk in the same way in which he walked.

7. All six occurrences are in the First Epistle of John: 2:29; 3:9; 4:7; 5:1, 4, 18.
8. 1 John 1:2, 3; 2:1, 13, 15–16, 22–24; 3:1; 4:14; 5:1.
9. 1 John 3:1, 2, 10; 5:2.
10. Law, *Tests of Life*, 208.

The "know" in 2:3 is γινώσκομεν as opposed to οἴδαμεν, which signifies an intimate experiential knowledge instead of a head knowledge.[11] Verses 5–6 teach that the way believers may *continuously* know (γινώσκομεν)[12] they are in a state of grace is that they *continuously* walk (περιπατεῖν)[13] in the same way Jesus walked (περιεπάτησεν). Nevertheless, no one can walk as perfectly as Jesus because John himself said earlier in 1:8, "If we say we have no sin, we deceive ourselves, and the truth is not in us." Therefore, if one component of assurance depends on believers' obedient walking as Jesus walked, this assurance is never perfect or infallible. This conclusion is consistent with WCF 18.4, which says, "True believers may have the assurance of their salvation divers ways shaken, diminished, and intermitted."

The second principal passage for the test of righteousness, stating negatively who the children of the devil are, is 3:4–10:

> *3:4* Everyone who makes a practice of sinning also practices lawlessness; sin is lawlessness. *5* You know that he appeared in order to take away sins, and in him there is no sin. *6* No one who abides in him keeps on sinning; no one who keeps on sinning has either seen him or known him. *7* Little children, let no one deceive you. Whoever practices righteousness is righteous, as he is righteous. *8* Whoever makes a practice of sinning is of the devil, for the devil has been sinning from the beginning. The reason the Son of God appeared was to destroy the works of the devil. *9* No one born of God makes a practice of sinning, for God's seed abides in him, and he cannot keep on sinning because he has been born of God. *10* By this it is evident who are the children of God, and who are the children of the devil: whoever does not practice righteousness is not of God, nor is the one who does not love his brother.

In this pericope, the litmus test that a person is of the devil is that he or she "makes a practice of sinning" (ποιῶν τὴν ἁμαρτίαν),[14] or "keeps on sinning" (ἁμαρτάνει),[15] or "practices lawlessness" (ποιῶν . . . ἀνομίαν),[16] or

11. Bass, *That You May Know*, 126.

12. This knowing is not a one-time event but a continuous knowing due to the present active indicative verb γινώσκομεν.

13. This "walk" is present active infinitive indicating a continuous doing what Jesus had done.

14. The original phrase in Greek occurs at 3:4, 8. A similar phrase (ἁμαρτίαν . . . ποιεῖ) occurs at 3:9. Literally, it is "keeps on doing sin," emphasizing that it is a habitual and recurring sin.

15. The original Greek occurs at 3:6, 8, indicating sinning as a lifestyle.

16. Practicing lawlessness is equivalent to practicing sin because "sin is lawlessness"

does not "practice righteousness" (μὴ ποιῶν δικαιοσύνην).[17] While the emphasis in 2:3–6 is on a believer's abiding in Jesus and following his footsteps, the present pericope stresses that such a believer neither practices sin nor lives a lifestyle of sin.

2. The Test of Love

The second cardinal test is the test of love,[18] especially the love for believers in the community of faith, as stated in 4:7, "Beloved, let us love one another, for love is from God, and whoever loves has been born of God and knows God." The relevant passages of this test include 2:9–11; 3:10–24; 4:7–13, 15–21; and 5:1–2. The central passage is 2:9–11:

> 2:9 Whoever says he is in the light and hates his brother is still in darkness. 10 Whoever loves his brother abides in the light, and in him there is no cause for stumbling. 11 But whoever hates his brother is in the darkness and walks in the darkness, and does not know where he is going, because the darkness has blinded his eyes.

Here, 2:9 exposes the lies of the one who says he is in the light when he is not because he hates (μισῶν)[19] his brother. Then, 2:10 says whoever loves (ἀγαπῶν) his brother abides (μένει) in the light.[20] Conversely, 2:11 says whoever hates (μισῶν) his brother walks (περιπατεῖ) in darkness.[21] Love of one's brother, or the lack thereof, is an indicator of whether one is in the light. The strong dualistic language of 2:9–11 suggests that the secessionists are walking in darkness despite their claims to the contrary because they hate John's readers.[22] Another key passage for the test of love is 3:11–20:

> 3:11 For this is the message that you have heard from the beginning, that we should love one another. 12 We should not be like Cain, who was of the evil one and murdered his brother.

(ἡ ἁμαρτία ἐστὶν ἡ ἀνομία) as stated in 3:4.

17. Both 3:7 and 3:10 use present active participle ποιῶν with respect to δικαιοσύνην.

18. Law, *Tests of Life*, 231.

19. The word "hate" is a present active participle, indicating a continuous action of hating.

20. "Loves" is a present active participle while "abides" is a present active indicative verb.

21. As in 2:10, "hates" is present active participle while "walks" is present active indicative.

22. Bass, *That You May Know*, 146.

And why did he murder him? Because his own deeds were evil and his brother's righteous. *13 Do not be surprised, brothers, that the world hates you. 14 We know that we have passed out of death into life, because we love the brothers.* Whoever does not love abides in death. *15* Everyone who hates his brother is a murderer, and you know that no murderer has eternal life abiding in him. *16* By this we know love, that he laid down his life for us, and we ought to lay down our lives for the brothers. *17* But if anyone has the world's goods and sees his brother in need, yet closes his heart against him, how does God's love abide in him? *18* Little children, let us not love in word or talk but in deed and in truth. *19* By this we shall know that we are of the truth and reassure our heart before him; *20* for whenever our heart condemns us, God is greater than our heart, and he knows everything.

This passage further reiterates love as the barometer of one's spiritual status before God. Verse 14 states that we know (οἴδαμεν) we have passed out of death into life because we love (ἀγαπῶμεν) the brothers. This knowledge is the assurance of salvation based on the continuous action of loving believers. This assurance, like the assurance of obedient walking, is also imperfect and fallible.

3. The Test of Belief

The test of belief is a test of truth to examine whether a person confesses Jesus as the Christ, the Son of God.[23] The pertinent passages include 2:18–27; 4:1–4, 15; and 5:1, 5–6. The following are the principal passages related to this truth test:

2:22 Who is the liar but he who denies that Jesus is the Christ? This is the antichrist, he who denies the Father and the Son. *23* No one who denies the Son has the Father. Whoever confesses the Son has the Father also.

4:2 By this you know the Spirit of God: every spirit that confesses that Jesus Christ has come in the flesh is from God, *3* and every spirit that does not confess Jesus is not from God. This is the spirit of the antichrist, which you heard was coming and now is in the world already.

---

23. Law, *Tests of Life*, 258.

5:5 Who is it that overcomes the world except the one who believes that Jesus is the Son of God?

The Greek word for "denies" in 2:22–23 is ἀρνούμενος, which is a
present middle participle. It signifies the continuous self-denial of Jesus as
Christ. It is not a one-time denial at a moment of weakness, like Peter's
denial of Jesus. Similarly, the Greek word for "confesses" in 4:2 is ὁμολογεῖ,
which is present active indicative. A true believer continues to confess Jesus
as having come in the flesh.

Furthermore, the Greek word for "believes" in 5:5 is πιστεύων, which is
a present active participle, indicating a continuous believing in Jesus as the
Son of God. These passages suggest that there is an intellectual component
of saving faith. True saving faith involves truthful confession of the identity
and person of Jesus: acknowledging Jesus as the Christ who came in the flesh.
The boundary between true believers (i.e., John's readers) and false ones (i.e.,
John's opponents) could not be more transparent. The former group professes
Jesus as the Christ (5:1), the latter denies it (2:22); the former acknowledges
Jesus as the Son (2:23; 3:23; 5:11) or the Son of God (1:3, 7; 3:8, 23; 4:9, 10,
15), the latter denies it (2:23); the former declares Jesus as having come in the
flesh (4:2),[24] the latter denies it.[25] This test is different from the other two as it
requires an intellectual consent to who Jesus is.

4. An Analysis of the Three Tests

These three tests, says Richard Phillips, intend to "inspire assurance in those
with a credible faith, not to inflict doubt on those with an imperfect faith."[26]
An analysis of these tests is instructive.

First, it would be fitting to reorder the three tests based on their prior-
ity, namely the tests of belief, righteousness, and love.[27] The reason is that
the test of belief holds primary importance as it is grounded in the identity
and person of Jesus—who is the Christ, the Son of God, and the One who
came in the flesh. If a person fails this belief test but passes the other two
tests, that person is still not a true believer.

24. That Jesus Christ came "by water and blood" (5:6) also indirectly affirms that
Jesus has come in the flesh.

25. This is recorded in 2 John 7: "For many deceivers have gone out into the world,
those who do not confess the coming of Jesus Christ in the flesh. Such a one is the
deceiver and the antichrist."

26. Phillips, "Assured in Christ," 84.

27. D. A. Carson calls these three tests as "truth test," "moral test," and "social test."
Carson, "Johannine Perspectives on Assurance," 67.

Second, only the test of belief is an objective test as its basis is on the finished work of Christ at the cross, as revealed in Scripture (1 Cor 15:3–4). It is a historical and unchangeable fact that Jesus came in the flesh, died on the cross, and arose on the third day. The other two tests are subjective in the sense that their basis is on the fruits of the Christians. Since fruits vary from person to person and from season to season, they are not an objective basis of assurance. The most subjective test of the three is the test of love because while the command to love is absolute, the expression of that love is relative.[28]

Third, since having the right knowledge is a prerequisite of right living, there is a causal progression in the three tests. It starts with an intellectual consent to fundamental doctrinal truth on Jesus' deity and humanity, which becomes the foundation of the subsequent tests of righteousness and love. The test of righteousness, which is a test of obedience to biblical truths, in turn, forms the foundation of the test of love. That is because love is the supreme fulfillment of the law (1 John 4:7–12; Gal 5:14; Rom 13:10). The test of righteousness emphasizes not doing evil; the test of love stresses doing good.

Fourth, there is also a progression in kinds as a person moves from the first test to the third test. The first test is ontological because it tests a person's understanding of essential truths. The other two tests are phenomenological. The test of righteousness is related to sins of commission—whether a person practices something that is forbidden by the law—that is, practices lawlessness as in 3:4. The test of love is about sins of omission—whether a person actively pursues a course of action that is commanded—in this case, love as Jesus loved. John's view of assurance, as seen from the last two tests, is not only regeneration-centric but also sanctification-centric. The tests of righteousness and love involve the fruits of a changed life as a result of regeneration.

Fifth, there is also a qualitative as well as a quantitative difference as one compares the first test to the other two tests. The first test is qualitative or digital. A person either believes Jesus as the Christ or not, or believes him as the Son of God or not—there is no middle ground. In contrast, the latter two tests are quantitative. People undoubtedly can have variable degrees of obedience and love.

Finally, as demonstrated by the main passages cited, there is an overwhelming use of present active indicative finite verbs and present active participles in the three tests. It means that leading a confessional, righteous,

---

28. Different cultures express love differently. An expression of love in one culture may well be interpreted as disrespect in another culture.

and loving life is a lifestyle, not a one-time past event. It is a present continuous habit that characterizes a healthy Christian life.

The three tests, in other words, are inherently tied to the perseverance of the saints. However, perseverance is not a fourth, independent test because it is inherent in the three tests. Nonetheless, one can conclude that the apostle John's view of assurance centers on regeneration, sanctification, and perseverance, which complements the apostle Paul's adoption-centric view of assurance.

5. The Fourth Test: The Test of the Witness of the Spirit

Upon a careful reading of 1 John, there exists evidence for an additional test not covered by the three tests proposed by Robert Law. This fourth test is the witness of the Spirit. The principal passages are the following:

> 3:24 Whoever keeps his commandments abides in God, and God in him. And by this we know that he abides in us, *by the Spirit whom he has given us.*

> 4:13 By this we know that we abide in him and he in us, *because he has given us of his Spirit.*

> 5:6 This is he who came by water and blood—Jesus Christ; not by the water only but by the water and the blood. *And the Spirit is the one who testifies*, because the Spirit is the truth. 7 For there are three that testify: *8 the Spirit and the water and the blood; and these three agree. 9* If we receive the testimony of men, the testimony of God is greater, for this is the testimony of God that he has borne concerning his Son. *10* Whoever believes in the Son of God has the testimony in himself. Whoever does not believe God has made him a liar, because he has not believed in the testimony that God has borne concerning his Son. *11* And this is the testimony, that God gave us eternal life, and this life is in his Son. *12* Whoever has the Son has life; whoever does not have the Son of God does not have life.

The first verse, 3:24, is in the broader context of love (3:11–24). However, 3:24 explicitly states that it is "by [ἐκ] the Spirit whom he has given us" that we continuously know (γινώσκομεν) he (i.e., God) abides in us. It is not by believers' love for one another that they know God abides in them, but by the witness of the Spirit in them. It is the Spirit-enabled experiential knowing, therefore, that provides the assurance. This verse links holy living with the work of the Holy Spirit as it is the Spirit who "touches our consciences with hungering and thirsting for advance, and these are evidence that we are saved."[29]

D. A. Carson's argument that 3:24 heralds the next section of 4:1–6 is not convincing. Based on 3:24, he claims, "The way one recognizes the presence of the Spirit of God is by a critical Christological confession."[30] The context, however, suggests that 3:24 belongs to the section of 3:11–24 on loving one another instead of 4:1–6 on testing the spirits. The critical phrase "keeps his commandments" in 3:24 also repeats in 3:22 and 23, yet it never occurs in 4:1–6. Another keyword "abides" in 3:24 also appears in 3:14 and 17, but not in 4:1–6. Besides, the second part of 3:24 connects to the first part by "and" (καὶ) but does not attach to the subsequent section. Moreover, the phrase "abides in us" (μένει ἐν ἡμῖν) in 3:24b organically links to "abides in God, and God in him" (ἐν αὐτῷ μένει καὶ αὐτὸς ἐν αὐτῷ·) in 3:24a. For these reasons, believers' experience of the Spirit constitutes another independent support of assurance, and it is not merely a manifestation of the observable work of the Spirit in the public arena, as argued by Carson.

The second principal verse, 4:13, is also in the broader context of love (4:7–21). Like 3:24, the rationale of 4:13 is "because he has given us of his Spirit" so we can continuously know (γινώσκομεν) "we abide in him and he in us." This abiding is mutual and two-way, as opposed to just one-way as in 3:24. Again, Christians know this mutual abiding not because they love one another, but because they have the Spirit.

The third passage, 5:6–12, is in the context of testimony concerning the Son of God.[31] In 5:6–8, the Spirit testifies that Jesus came by water and blood, which has reference to Jesus' baptism and his crucifixion, respectively.[32] The present tense of the verb "testifies" (μαρτυροῦν) in "the Spirit testifies" indicates that this testimony is an inner witness of the Spirit, which is ongoing.[33] If one analyzes the flow of 5:6–12, this testimony of the Spirit to the historicity of Jesus' public ministry, climaxing at his death, is an essential component of the testimony of God (μαρτυρία τοῦ θεοῦ) concerning his Son (5:9).

29. Masters, *Faith, Doubts, Trials*, 103.

30. Carson, "Johannine Perspectives on Assurance," 72–73.

31. A contextual analysis shows that 5:1–5 speaks of the experiential aspect of the saving faith, whereas 5:6–12 focuses on the object and the content of that faith. Specifically, the object is Jesus Christ, and the content is his redemptive work initiated by his baptism and climaxed at his crucifixion.

32. His coming by water would then mark the beginning of his ministry, as his coming by blood (i.e., his death) marked its end. Kruse, *Letters of John*, 175.

33. Burge, *Letters of John*, 203.

John goes on to define what this testimony is in 5:11–12: "And this is the testimony, that God gave us eternal life, and this life is in his Son. Whoever has the Son has life; whoever does not have the Son of God does not have life." The Spirit-wrought testimony is, therefore, concerning God's Son, and whoever receives that testimony can be sure God has given him or her eternal life.

If one compares 5:11–12 with the testimony of the Spirit in Rom 8:16, where the Spirit himself bears witness with believers' spirit they are children of God, one can see the primary difference between the testimony spoken of by Paul and John. In the case of Paul, the Spirit testifies with believers' spirit they are (plural) children of God. For John, the Spirit testifies that each believer has eternal life. Each person, John emphasizes, must be born again to enter God's family. Paul highlights the communal, rather than the individual, aspect of the adopted children of God when they collectively cry out, "Abba! Father!" (Rom 8:15).

John stresses the new life (through regeneration) and the fruits thereof (through sanctification) because Jesus came so his sheep may have life and have it more abundantly (John 10:10). Since the Spirit's testimony is ongoing, this alludes to the perseverance of the saints. Once again, John's view of assurance centers on the birth of the new life (regeneration), the growth of that life (sanctification), and the endurance of it (perseverance).

Paul, on the other hand, chooses adoption as the core illustration. This adoption is authored before creation, anticipated in the Old Testament, arrived in the Messiah, assured by the Spirit, and achieved in the *parousia*. Adoption is the thread through which the entire redemptive history, from election to glorification, is organically linked. Paul's adoption-centric view of assurance complements John's regeneration-centric, sanctification-centric, and perseverance-centric view.

At the end of the letter, John concludes his argument and states his purpose of writing the letter in 5:13, "I write these things to you who believe in the name of the Son of God that you may know that you have eternal life."

D. IS ASSURANCE OF THE ESSENCE OF FAITH?

Based on the textual evidence of the letter of 1 John, there are four grounds of assurance: orthodox belief in Jesus as the Christ, the Son of God, the one who came in the flesh; the obedient living according to biblical ethical standards; the love of fellow believers in action; and the inner testimony of the Spirit the person has eternal life.

The first ground is the objective confessional belief in the deity and humanity of Jesus, as revealed in Scripture. Though this ground of assurance is objective because its foundation is God's revelation, the intensity of this assurance still varies from person to person because people respond to the truth in different proportions. Sinclair Ferguson expresses it aptly:

> Faith seeks understanding and is nourished through it. It is possible, of course, to have little knowledge and yet real assurance because faith has nourished itself richly on the knowledge it possesses. Correspondingly, it is possible to have much knowledge and little assurance if an individual responds disproportionately to the knowledge he or she possesses.[34]

The second and third ground have subjective elements that are susceptible to variations and fluctuations in a person's intimate walk with God. Assurance, thus, is not a static entity but a dynamic one.[35] A Christian's assurance can, and should, grow over time. Concerning the subjective elements of assurance, Louis Berkhof comments that they belong to the "syllogism of faith" in which the first premise is furnished by Scripture and the second by the regenerated consciousness. The deductive reasoning goes as follows: "The Bible says that whosoever truly believeth is saved, and the Christian confesses that he is conscious of believing with a saving faith, and then draws the conclusion that he is therefore saved."[36] It is the second premise that is subjective because its basis is on self-examination whether the person has truly believed in the biblical sense. Since a believer in this life cannot achieve perfect sinlessness (1:8, 10; 2:1; 5:16–17), these two grounds contribute to the assurance of salvation in a supportive manner.

The fourth ground is the inner testimony of the Holy Spirit, which, as argued in the previous chapter, is both objective and subjective. Overall, under the greater regeneration-centric understanding of assurance by John, the first ground addresses the mind, the second and the third ground touch on the will, and the fourth ground speaks to the heart.

The ground of assurance and the ground of faith, one must note, should be distinguished—the two are related but not identical. The only ground of faith is the person and work of Jesus, accomplished through his death and

---

34. Ferguson, *Whole Christ*, 199.

35. Hoskinson, *Assurance of Salvation*, 216.

36. Berkhof, *Assurance of Faith*, 45. The Puritans further subdivided the "syllogism of faith" into the practical syllogism and the mystical syllogism. The former is concerned with external, objective, and observable evidence such as obedience and love; the latter deals with internal, subjective, and inward evidence such as delighting in God's words and prayers and longing for the return of Christ.

resurrection. Righteous living and loving one's fellow Christians can never become the ground of faith as salvation is only by grace alone, through faith alone, in Christ alone, and not of works (Eph 2:8–9).

In the final analysis, the first ground of assurance is the orthodox confession of Jesus as the Christ and the Son. It also entails the embracing of that confession as definite and personal knowledge. The second and third ground of assurance—a righteous and loving living—is the fruit of that faith, not the ground of faith or faith itself. The fourth ground of assurance, the work of the Holy Spirit, creates the supernatural spiritual rebirth of the sinner in the first place. The Spirit then imparts assurance, produces the fruits of faith that corroborate and confirm that assurance, and continuously testifies during believers' perseverance that they are children, born of God.

Hence, based on this analysis from 1 John, assurance, it must be concluded, is *not* of the essence of faith. In other words, genuine faith does not necessarily and automatically produce assurance, as assurance also depends on secondary and subjective grounds of righteous and loving living. That is also the reason why the apostle John writes the First Epistle of John in the first place, "I write these things to you who believe in the name of the Son of God, that you may know that you have eternal life."

E. SUMMARY

The apostle John's view of assurance centers on regeneration, sanctification, and perseverance. Assurance, at least infallible assurance, is not of the essence of faith as it comprises both an objective basis on the finished work of Christ and a subjective basis on righteous and loving living. The witness of the Holy Spirit seals in the hearts of believers that they are born of God through regeneration. The grounds of assurance are related to the grounds of faith, but they are not identical. In Part IV, we endeavor to understand assurance from the perspective of systematic theology.

PART IV

Theological Analysis

Chapter 7

Assurance and Union with Christ

Having already established that an adoption-centric view of assurance best captures the richness of salvation, or in short, assurance of adoption is assurance of salvation, the goal of this chapter is to defend the thesis that assurance itself is a redemptive benefit derived from union with Christ. The theological concept of union with Christ, as such, must first be grasped. This union entails covenantal solidarity between Christ and the elect, whereby the Spirit unites the elect to Christ through faith. This union forms the basis for the elect to receive *all* the benefits of redemption accomplished by Christ. Jesus saves the elect by uniting them to himself through the effectual calling of the Spirit.

A. UNION WITH CHRIST AS THE ORGANIZING PRINCIPLE OF REDEMPTIVE BENEFITS

Geerhardus Vos considers union with Christ as of primary significance in a Reformed understanding of salvation: "One is first united to Christ, the Mediator of the covenant, by a mystical union, which finds its conscious recognition in faith. By this union with Christ, all that is in Christ is simultaneously given."[1] In recent years, there has been a resurging interest in the doctrine of union with Christ, as judged by the number of monographs,

---

1. Vos, "Doctrine of the Covenant," 256.

book chapters, and journal articles published.[2] One of the most impressive works is Constantine Campbell's book *Paul and Union with Christ*. Campbell meticulously studies each occurrence of the prepositional phrase ἐν Χριστῷ (in Christ),[3] εἰς Χριστόν (into Christ),[4] σὺν Χριστῷ (with Christ),[5] and διὰ Χριστοῦ (through Christ).[6] At the end of his laborious study of these phrases, and their intersections with theological concepts such as Trinity and justification, Campbell concludes that union with Christ entails four aspects:

> I propose that this theme is best conveyed through four terms: union, participation, identification, and incorporation. Union gathers up faith union with Christ, mutual indwelling, trinitarian, and nuptial notions. Participation conveys partaking in the events of Christ's narrative. Identification refers to believers' location in the realm of Christ and their allegiance to his lordship. Incorporation encapsulates the corporate dimension of membership in Christ's body. Together these four terms function as "umbrella" concepts, covering the full spectrum of Pauline language, ideas, and themes that are bound up in the metatheme of "union with Christ."[7]

2. Gaffin, "Union with Christ"; Gaffin, "Justification and Union with Christ"; Tipton, "Union with Christ and Justification"; Garcia, *Life in Christ*; Billings, "John Calvin: United to God"; Billings, "John Calvin's Soteriology"; Billings, *Union with Christ*; Horton, *Covenant and Salvation*; Evans, *Imputation and Impartation;* Venema, "Union with Christ"; Smedes, *Union with Christ*; Letham, *Union with Christ*; Campbell, *Paul and Union with Christ*; Fesko, *Beyond Calvin*; Johnson, *One with Christ*; Fitzpatrick, *Found in Him*; Macaskill, *Union with Christ*; Peterson, *Salvation Applied by the Spirit*.

3. According to Campbell, there is no discernible difference in function between ἐν Χριστῷ, ἐν κυρίῳ, ἐν αὐτῷ, and ἐν ᾧ. These phrases, he discovers, are found "in reference to things achieved for/given to people, believers' actions, characteristics of believers, faith in Christ, justification and new status." Campbell, *Paul and Union with Christ*, 198–99.

4. Campbell demonstrates, in many cases, an overlap in the semantic range between εἰς Χριστόν and ἐν Χριστῷ, but εἰς αὐτόν in two instances denotes the concept of union with Christ. The most common usage of εἰς is "the expression of goal and reference or respect." Campbell, *Paul and Union with Christ*, 215–16.

5. Most occurrences of the σὺν-compound variations, Campbell notes, denote participation with Christ as believers partake with Christ in his death, burial, resurrection, ascension, and session. Campbell, *Paul and Union with Christ*, 236.

6. The phrase διὰ Χριστοῦ signifies mostly instrumentality and sometimes *mediatorial* as in "Christ mediates the action of another." Campbell cites examples of such action of God in creation (1 Cor 8:6; Col 1:16), the revelation of salvation and reconciliation (2 Cor 5:18; Col 1:20), and the impartation of the Spirit (Titus 3:6). Campbell, *Paul and Union with Christ*, 266.

7. Campbell, *Paul and Union with Christ*, 413.

Putting union with Christ under a more soteriological light, Wayne Grudem succinctly summarizes the doctrine in the following:

> Union with Christ is a phrase used to summarize several different relationships between believers and Christ, through which Christians receive every benefit of salvation. These relationships include the fact that we are in Christ, Christ is in us, we are like Christ, and we are with Christ.[8]

With this understanding, the notion of union with Christ means that a person must be *in* Christ to partake of any redemptive benefit merited *by* Christ. This union underlies all the redemptive blessings not only of justification and sanctification but also adoption, perseverance, and glorification. All these spiritual blessings in the heavenly places manifest union with Christ through Spirit-wrought faith. A person is justified because that person is in union with Christ, not vice versa. Ferguson calls union with Christ in the Spirit as the "dominant motif and architectonic principle of the order of salvation."[9] It follows that assurance, being one of the benefits and a by-product of salvation, also necessarily derives from union with Christ.

B. UNION WITH CHRIST IN THE HISTORICAL CONTEXT

The doctrine of union with Christ occupies a central position in the thought of the Reformers and Puritans. John Calvin, underscoring the centrality of this doctrine, famously says, "As long as Christ remains outside of us, and we are separated from him, all that he has suffered and done for the salvation of the human race remains useless and of no value for us."[10] This union, Calvin further asserts, is brought about by "the secret energy of the Spirit, by which we come to enjoy Christ and all his benefits."[11]

The Puritan theologian John Owen (1616–83), in his Two Short Catechisms Chapter XXI—"Of the Privileges of Believers," asks the following at the outset.[12]

Q. 1: What are the privileges of those that thus believe and repent?

---

8. Grudem, *Systematic Theology*, 840.

9. Ferguson, *Holy Spirit*, 100.

10. Calvin, *Institutes.* 3.1.1 (537).

11. Calvin, *Institutes.* 3.1.1 (537).

12. Owen, *Works of John Owen*, 489.

A. 1: First, *union with Christ*; secondly, adoption of children; thirdly, Christian liberty; fourthly, spiritual, holy right to the seals of the new covenant; fifthly, communion of all saints; sixthly, resurrection of the body unto life eternal.

Q. 2: What is our union with Christ?

A. 2: An holy, spiritual conjunction onto him, as our head, husband, and foundation, whereby we are made partakers of the same Spirit with him and derive all good things from him.

Union with Christ, as Owen's response to Q. 1 indicates, is not only the basis of all the redemptive benefits, as Calvin teaches, but is itself the foremost benefit. Moreover, adoption is listed immediately after union with Christ, so it manifests and is subordinate to the union, which is not only the overarching benefit, as his response to Q. 2 shows, but the fountainhead of all other benefits.

In WLC Q. 65–66, the following is stated:

Q. 65: What special benefits do the members of the invisible church enjoy by Christ?

A. 65: The members of the invisible church, by Christ, enjoy union and communion with him in grace and glory.[13]

Q. 66: What is that union which the elect have with Christ?

A. 66: The union which the elect have with Christ is the work of God's grace,[1] whereby they are spiritually and mystically, yet really and inseparably, joined to Christ as their head and husband;[2] which is done in their effectual calling.[3][14]

The Westminster divines consider union and communion with Christ, as A. 65 shows, as the exclusive benefit believers enjoy; no other benefits, not even adoption or the "double grace" of justification and sanctification, are mentioned. Furthermore, this union with Christ, as seen from A. 66, is achieved by effectual calling, which ushers in the rest of the redemptive benefits of justification, adoption, sanctification, perseverance, and glorification. Q. and A. 69 further state:

Q. 69: What is the communion in grace which the members of the invisible church have with Christ?

---

13. John 17:21, 24; Eph 2:5–6.

14. [1] Eph 1:22; 2:67. [2] 1 Cor 6:17; John 10:28; Eph 5:23, 30. [3] 1 Pet 5:10; 1 Cor 1:9.

A. 69: The communion in grace which the members of the invisible church have with Christ, is their partaking of the virtue of his mediation, in their justification,[1] adoption,[2] sanctification, and whatever else, in this life, manifests their union with him.[3]15

A. 69 delineates the relationship between union with Christ and the communion in grace whereby the latter, consisting of all the redemptive benefits, is a manifestation of the former. Since all redemptive benefits manifest union with Christ, this doctrine is Christological (Christ-centered) as it exalts Christ, the benefactor of salvation, instead of the redeemed, the beneficiaries of salvation, much less the benefits of salvation.

C. UNION WITH CHRIST IN THE BIBLICAL CONTEXT

Union with Christ is not only a theological concept but a redemptive reality rooted in scriptural revelation. The phrase "union with Christ," like the term "Trinity," is not explicitly found in Scripture, yet the concept permeates the entire Bible.

1. Old Testament

The Scriptures, asserts Jesus, testify about him (John 5:39).[16] He tells the two disciples on the road to Emmaus, "Everything written about me in the Law of Moses and the Prophets and the Psalms must be fulfilled" (Luke 24:44). The core testimony of all the prophets have spoken and predicted is that "Christ should suffer these things and enter into his glory" (Luke 24:25–26; 1 Pet 1:10–12). At the heart of the prophetic corpus of the Old Testament is the promise of a coming messiah through whose sufferings God would establish a people for himself. The sacrifice of the suffering messiah would usher in a new era, and indeed a new covenant, in which an intimate relationship between God and his people would emerge. Jeremiah prophesies this new covenant:

> Behold, the days are coming, declares the LORD, when I will make a new covenant with the house of Israel and the house of Judah, not like the covenant that I made with their fathers on the day when I took them by the hand to bring them out of the land of Egypt, my covenant that they broke, though I was their husband, declares the LORD. For this is the covenant that I will make with the house of Israel after those days, declares the

15. [1] Rom 8:30. [2] Eph 1:5. [3] 1 Cor 1:30.
16. The Scriptures in view are the Old Testament we now have.

LORD: I will put my law within them, and I will write it on their hearts. And I will be their God, and they shall be my people. And no longer shall each one teach his neighbor and each his brother, saying, "Know the LORD," for they shall all know me, from the least of them to the greatest, declares the LORD. For I will forgive their iniquity, and I will remember their sin no more. (Jer 31:31–34)

This new covenant is none other than the administration of the covenant of grace under the New Testament economy. The term of this new covenant is that Jesus, as the Messiah anticipated by the Jews, would die for the sins of his people who, through faith, can participate in him and all the redemptive benefits accomplished by the Messiah.

Moses prophesies about this new covenant in Deut 30:6: "And the LORD your God will circumcise your heart and the heart of your offspring, so that you will love the LORD your God with all your heart and with all your soul, that you may live." The prophet Ezekiel also anticipates the new covenant in Ezek 36:26–27: "And I will give you a new heart, and a new spirit I will put within you. And I will remove the heart of stone from your flesh and give you a heart of flesh. And I will put my Spirit within you, and cause you to walk in my statutes and be careful to obey my rules." The prophet Isaiah presents a clear picture on the mission of the suffering messiah in Isa 53:5: "But he was pierced for our transgressions; he was crushed for our iniquities; upon him was the chastisement that brought us peace, and with his wounds we are healed." It is through the substitutionary death of the messiah that God can reconcile his people to him, and the promise of "I will be your God, and you shall be my people" can be realized. The concept of union with the messiah, as these and other passages in the Old Testament indicate, is at the center of the Old Testament revelation.

2. New Testament

In the New Testament, at last, this new covenant spoken by the prophets was instituted by Jesus at the Last Supper when he told his disciples: "This is my body, which is given for you. Do this in remembrance of me. . . . This cup that is poured out for you is the new covenant in my blood" (Luke 22:19–20). The new covenant officially took effect when Jesus, the testator of the new covenant, died a bloody death on the cross (Heb 9:16–17). People can participate in this new covenant only through faith in Jesus the Messiah.

Paul in Rom 5:12–21 provides the theological underpinning of union with Christ based on a representative principle. There exist, Paul argues, two parallel representative relationships, one between Adam and all his posterity, the other between Christ, the second Adam, and the new humanity he came to redeem. Even as Adam, the federal representative head and the biological progenitor of all humanity, imputed his initial sin and its guilt to all humanity, so Christ, the federal representative head of the elect, imputes his righteousness and obedience to those who by faith are united to him. The redemptive event of the death and resurrection of Jesus, the Mediator of the covenant of grace, forms the basis of union with Christ.

Paul, in Rom 6:1–11, presents another dimension of this union with Christ. Not only did Christ die and rise again *for* his people, but his people also died and rose *with* him. The elect, through their union with Christ, participate in the historical death and resurrection of Christ. Their union with Christ, consequently, is not only representative but solidaric.

Because of believers' solidarity with Christ's death, they are to consider themselves "dead [ἀπεθάνομεν] to sin" because all those who have been "baptized [ἐβαπτίσθημεν] into Christ Jesus" were "baptized [ἐβαπτίσθημεν] into his death" and were "buried [συνετάφημεν] with him" by baptism into his death (Rom 6:2–4). Truly, the believers' old man, being in union with Adam and consequently subjected to the dominion of sin and death, was "crucified [συνεσταυρώθη] with Christ" (6:6) and "died [ἀπεθάνομεν] with Christ" (6:8). The persistent and conspicuous use of the aorist indicative first person plural in these verses denotes a completed, decisive action in the past in which believers were dead with Christ and buried with him.[17]

Believers, furthermore, are also in solidarity with Christ's resurrection. Just as Christ rose from the dead, so believers too might walk in newness of life (6:4) because they shall be united with him in a resurrection like his (6:5), and they will also live with him (6:8).[18] The resurrection of Jesus, Sinclair Ferguson convincingly argues, is his justification (1 Tim 3:16), adoption (Rom 1:3–4), sanctification (Rom 6:9–10), and glorification (1 Cor 15:20).[19] On account of Christ's resurrection, he is justified in the sense of being vindicated, adopted in the sense of being manifested as the Son of God in power, sanctified as having been dead to sins once for all and now lives to God, and glorified by having received a real resurrected body, which believers will also receive when Christ returns in glory.

To be united to Christ is to participate in all Christ has accomplished by his death and resurrection. All Christ has achieved—justification, adoption,

17. Key passages that speak of believers dying with Christ are Gal 2:20; Col 2:11–12; and 2 Cor 5:14.

18. Other passages on believers being resurrected with Christ are Gal 2:19–20; Col 2:12; 3:1; and Eph 2:4–5.

19. Ferguson, *Holy Spirit*, 104–6.

sanctification, and glorification—believers can participate through union with Christ by Spirit-created faith. Paul does not mean, of course, that believers physically died and rose with Christ in a subjective sense. Nevertheless, Paul shows that this union with Christ is so real that the elect, being in solidarity with Christ and represented by him, did die in his death and rise in his resurrection in an objective sense. Because of the historical death and resurrection of Jesus, believers in their existential Christian life are to consider themselves as having died to sin and risen again to walk in newness of life (Rom 6:11).

Believers, through union with Christ, also share in his ascension and session. After describing believers as having died and been raised with Christ in Eph 2:5, Paul in verses 6–7 says, "[God] raised us up with him and seated us with him in the heavenly places in Christ Jesus, so that in the coming ages he might show the immeasurable riches of his grace in kindness toward us in Christ Jesus." Calvin, in his commentary on Eph 2:6, says:

> The resurrection and sitting in heaven, which are here mentioned, are not yet seen by mortal eyes. Yet, as if those blessings were presently in our possession, he states that we have received them; and illustrates the change which has taken place in our condition when we were led from Adam to Christ. It is as if we had been brought from the deepest hell to heaven itself.[20]

Paul continues to explain the theological significance of the ascension and session in Eph 4:8–10. There, because of his ascension, Christ spoiled his enemies and distributed the gifts to the church. These gifts include "the apostles, the prophets, the evangelists, the shepherds and teachers" (4:11). The connection between believers' union with Christ and Christ's session is reiterated in Col 3:1: "If then you have been raised with Christ, seek the things that are above, where Christ is, seated at the right hand of God." As such, new-covenant believers, unlike old-covenant saints, are united to an exalted Christ, not a Christ yet to come.

Through union with Christ, believers are united to Christ redemptive-historically in his life, death, burial, resurrection, ascension, and session. Everything Christ has experienced believers would also have experienced, in an objective sense, through their union with him. For this reason, Paul concludes in 1 Cor 1:30, "And because of him you are in Christ Jesus, who became to us wisdom from God, righteousness and sanctification and redemption."

---

20. Calvin, *Commentary on Ephesians*, 225.

3. Biblical Illustrations

The New Testament writers use different examples and illustrations to elucidate the meaning of union with Christ. The first is the *divine* union of God the Father and the Son wherein the Father is in the Son and the Son in the Father, and they are one (John 10:30; 14:10–11). This divine union is the highest and most ideal model of union and is also an eternal reality in the Godhead. The second example is the union between Christ and the church (Col 1:18; Eph 5:32; 2 Cor 11:2; Rev 19:7; 21:9). This *spiritual* union with Christ is both an illustration and a reality. The third illustration, in the realm of marriage, is the *marital* union between husband and wife (Mark 10:6–9; Eph 5:22–31). The fourth, in physiology, entails the *physical* union between the head and members making up the body (Eph 4:15–16). The fifth, an agricultural illustration, consists of the *organic* union between the vine and branches (John 15:1–6). The last one, in architecture, illustrates the *structural* union between the cornerstone and other stones that made up the building (1 Cor 3:11; Eph 2:19–22; 1 Pet 2:4–8).

D. UNION WITH CHRIST AND THE *ORDO SALUTIS*

The *ordo salutis* (Latin for "order of salvation") refers to elements of salvation arranged logically from the perspective of the redeemed. The best scriptural example of an *ordo salutis* is Rom 8:30: "And those whom he predestined he also called, and those whom he called he also justified, and those whom he justified he also glorified." This verse is the basis of the so-called "golden chain."[21] It is a shortened *ordo* that nonetheless includes the pivotal elements in a logical order: predestination, effectual calling, justification, and glorification. Table 6 arranges the elements of the *ordo* in the Reformed tradition.

---

21. The term "golden chain" is coined from the systematic theological work of William Perkins, *Golden Chain*.

Table 6: The *ordo salutis* in the Reformed tradition.

Band	The Ordo Salutis	Meaning	Scripture Reference
1	Election	Choose people for salvation	Eph 1:4; Rom 9:11; 2 Tim 1:9
	Predestination	Ordain the elect for adoption	1 Cor 2:7; Eph 1:5
2	Effectual Calling	Quicken the elect	1 Cor 1:9; Rom 8:29–30; 2 Tim 1:9
	Regeneration	Born again by the Spirit and the word	John 3:3–8; Ezek 36:25–27; Eph 2:4–5; Col 2:13; Tit 3:4–7
	Conversion	Repent and believe	Ezek 18:30–32; John 3:16; Rom 5:1; Eph 2:8
	Justification	Forgive all sins	Rom 3:25–26, 4:5; 8:1; 1 Cor 1:30; 2 Cor 5:21
	Adoption	Adopt as God's children	Rom 8:14–17; Eph 1:5; John 1:12; Gal 4:5
	Definitive Sanctification	Break from sin's enslavement and are called saints	Rom 6:1–11; 1 Cor 6:11
3	Progressive Sanctification	Grow in holiness	Rom 6:12–23; Gal 5:22–23; 1 Pet 1:5–8
	Perseverance	Continue in the faith	John 10:28–29; Rom 8:31–39; 1 Cor 1:4–9; Heb 7:25; 1 Pet 1:3–5
4	Glorification	Receive resurrected body	1 Cor 15:50–53; Rom 8:23, 30

All parts of the *ordo* are distinct yet inseparable, but union with Christ undergirds the entire spectrum of salvation. Union with Christ, assuredly, is the alpha and omega of the *ordo*. It starts with the election in Christ by the Father, and it ends with believers in glorification in Christ. Union with Christ, however, is not listed as one of the elements of the *ordo* because it encompasses the entire gamut of the *ordo*. All parts of the *ordo* are originated and derived from union with Christ, which is an umbrella rubric that embraces all the spiritual blessings of salvation. The union is thus a case in which the whole (union with Christ) is greater than the sum of its parts (salvation benefits in the *ordo*).

Union with Christ, hence, is more than the totality of all redemptive benefits. Not only does it precede any element in the *ordo*, but it is also the very fountain out of which all the benefits of redemption flow, including assurance of salvation. Union with Christ is the divine basis upon which a person can receive saving grace. As far as the application of redemption is concerned, "nothing is more central or basic," John Murray asserts, "than union or communion with Christ."[22] He further says:

> Union with Christ is in itself a very broad and embracive subject. It is not simply a step in the application of redemption; . . . it underlies every step of the application of redemption. Union with Christ is really the central truth of the whole doctrine of salvation not only in its application but also in its once-for-all accomplishment in the finished work of Christ. Indeed the whole process of salvation has its origin in one phase of union with Christ and salvation has in view the realization of other phases of union with Christ.[23]

From the perspective of time, the *ordo* has temporal aspects, starting from past eternity to future eternity. Even though there is not a strict chronological sequence between successive elements in the *ordo*, there is a temporal sequence among successive bands of elements in the *ordo*.

The first band of elements, election and predestination, are pretemporal and, in fact, atemporal. It is because believers are elected or chosen by God in him (ἐν αὐτῷ, i.e., Christ) before the foundation of the world to be predestined for adoption as sons through Jesus (Eph 1:4–5). Election and predestination are outside time and are being carried out by the eternal, hidden decrees of God. Before the foundation of the world, God in his omniscience already saw the elect—still yet to be created—and chose them in Christ. In particular, from eternity past, members of the Trinity enter into a covenant of redemption or *pactum salutis*.[24]

This covenant is Trinitarian. It entails the Father giving to the Son those whom he chose to save. It also necessitates that the Son agrees, as the federal representative head of the elect, to pay for their sins. The Son, as such, needs to become a man through incarnation. He obligates himself to keep all the demands of the covenant of works on behalf of the elect. Besides, he must receive the imputation of the sins of the elect to himself for which he would incur the divine punishment in his vicarious and substitutionary death. Only then can the Spirit apply to the elect the redemptive benefits earned by the Son through uniting the elect to the Son by faith.

The *pactum salutis* underlies the eternal origin of union with Christ. It is the driving force of the covenant of grace, which is nothing but the

22. Murray, *Redemption Accomplished and Applied*, 161.
23. Murray, *Redemption Accomplished and Applied*, 161.
24. It is also called "the counsel of peace"; see Fesko, *Covenant of Redemption*, 15.

historical outworking and unfolding of the *pactum salutis*, culminating in the death and resurrection of Christ. Louis Berkhof, speaking about *pactum salutis*, writes:

> In the counsel of peace Christ voluntarily took upon Himself to be the Head and Surety of the elect, destined to constitute the new humanity, and as such to establish their righteousness before God by paying the penalty for their sin and by rendering perfect obedience to the law and thus securing their title to everlasting life. In that eternal covenant the sin of His people was imputed to Christ, and His righteousness was imputed to them.[25]

The second band of elements in the *ordo salutis* consists of effectual calling, regeneration, conversion, justification, adoption, and definitive sanctification. They are past elements based on the historical work of Jesus, who, in the fullness of time, was incarnated, lived a life of perfect righteousness, died on the cross for the sins of the elect, rose on the third day, ascended into heaven, and is seated at the right hand of God. Then, in due time, the Holy Spirit, through the preaching of the gospel, effectually called the sinners. This effectual calling results in the regeneration of the elect, with repentance and faith as its fruits. Believers are then justified *sola fide*, adopted into God's family, and sanctified to be saints.

Some Reformed theologians are emphatic that repentance, unlike faith, comes after union with Christ. In this view, whereas faith is the instrumental bond that unites the elect to Christ, thus *a priori* to union with Christ, repentance is a fruit of union. For instance, Thomas Boston (1676–1732), the eighteenth-century Scottish Reformed theologian, says:

> Now, if union with Christ be the immediate effect of faith, repentance must either go before faith, or it must come after remission of sins. The former cannot be said, seeing the repentance in question is pleasing to God; but "without faith it is impossible to please God." The Lord himself tells us, that without him we can do nothing. . . . Now, we are still without Christ, till by faith we be united to him, Eph. 3:17. Wherefore true repentance cannot go before faith. It remains then, that it comes after remission of sin.[26]

Here, it is crucial to note that justification, adoption, and definitive sanctification are as decisive in their once-for-all character as they are

---

25. Berkhof, *Systematic Theology*, 378

26. Boston, *Complete Works*, 6:79.

eschatological. Carrying on the insights from the work of Herman Ridderbos and Geerhardus Vos,[27] Richard Gaffin persuasively argues that believers, in a sense, still await their justification because they have yet to receive their resurrected bodies, which will happen on Judgment Day. On that occasion, since believers are already righteous, they shall be "openly acknowledged and acquitted" as such.[28]

The Scripture also speaks of adoption in an eschatological sense because believers "wait eagerly for adoption as sons, the redemption of our bodies" (Rom 8:23). Adoption, as argued in chapter 2, is the highest and most comprehensive benefit encompassing the existential, judicial, relational, moral, and eschatological dimensions of salvation.

Similarly, definitive sanctification, as unrepeatable as the death and resurrection of Christ (Rom 6:1–11), is an accomplished act of God. That is the reason the apostle Paul can address believers as "you were washed, *you were sanctified* [ἡγιάσθητε], you were justified" (1 Cor 6:11). In this verse, sanctification, that is, definitive sanctification, precedes even justification.

The third band of elements, progressive sanctification and perseverance, are concurrent with the lives of believers. After God has definitively sanctified them, they are being progressively sanctified and kept in perseverance in the faith. Progressive sanctification and perseverance are gracious works of the Holy Spirit, who produces the fruit of the Spirit (Gal 5:22–23) and enjoins believers to persevere (2 Pet 1:5–13). Believers live with the eschatological hope that one day they will achieve perfect sanctification at death, which eventually culminates in bodily sanctification at glorification when they will receive their new resurrected bodies.

The last band is glorification, which is both a present and a future event. At present, God molds believers into the image of Christ, from glory to glory (2 Cor 3:18). Upon death, the souls of believers pass into heaven, which signals the beginning of everlasting joy. Finally, at Christ's second coming, believers will experience final glorification when they receive their glorified spiritual bodies (1 Cor 15:50–54), which is the traditional theological meaning of glorification.

A causal relationship exists, one can observe, between these bands of elements. The first band of elements, election and predestination, are outside time, but they propel the elements in the second band forward. What God the Father sets in eternity, the Son accomplished in history, and the Holy Spirit operated during the lifetime of the elect to effectually call them, which caused a chain reaction through regeneration, conversion, justification,

---

27. Ridderbos, *Paul*; Vos, *Biblical Theology*.

28. Gaffin, *By Faith, Not by Sight*, 93–94.

adoption, and definitive sanctification. Then, the third band of elements, progressive sanctification and perseverance, will run their course, eventually leading to glorification when Christ returns. To put it differently, while a temporal or logical relationship is hard to establish within the bands, it is evident that such a relationship exists between the bands.

E. UNION WITH CHRIST AND PENTECOST

The *ordo salutis* contains the elements of salvation for the *individual* believer, the basis of which is the union of that individual with Christ through Spirit-created faith. The New Testament also speaks of union with Christ in a corporate sense. The church, as a corporate body, is united to Christ by the outpouring of the Spirit of Christ. This corporate baptism happened, decisively, at Pentecost.

Before Jesus' public ministry, John the Baptist prophesied, "I baptize you with water for repentance, but he who is coming after me is mightier than I, whose sandals I am not worthy to carry. He will baptize you with the Holy Spirit and fire" (Matt 3:11). The next verse, "His winnowing fork is in his hand, and he will clear his threshing floor and gather his wheat into the barn, but the chaff he will burn with unquenchable fire," clearly indicates the fire spoken about is the eschatological judgment of God. The baptism of fire is thus a judgment Jesus must endure (Mark 10:38–39). This judgment materialized when Jesus, the sin-bearer of the elect, suffered the wrath of God for them at the cross.[29]

Then, fifty days after Jesus' resurrection, as the disciples were waiting for the promised Holy Spirit, "divided tongues as of fire appeared to them and rested on each one of them. And they were all filled with the Holy Spirit and began to speak in other tongues as the Spirit gave them utterance" (Acts 2:2–3). The fire of divine judgment at the cross has turned into the fire of spiritual cleansing and empowerment at Pentecost. That is a fulfillment of John the Baptist's prophecy—Jesus would baptize with the Holy Spirit and fire.

Pentecost signifies the official birth of the New Testament church in which Jesus cleansed the church by and filled her with the Spirit to make her sanctified and bold as Jesus' holy representative and witness on earth. Hence, the invisible, corporate, and universal church was officially born

---

29. Richard Gaffin interprets the baptism by fire, which is a judgment by God, as fulfilled in a two-stage process. First, in Jesus' baptism by John the Baptist, Jesus became identified with his people as their sin-bearer. Second, Jesus took on the judgment of his people and died vicariously at the cross. Gaffin, "Holy Spirit," 65–66.

when the promised Holy Spirit was poured out mightily at Pentecost.[30] On that occasion, Jesus poured out his Spirit as a fulfillment of the prophecy of Ezekiel—"I will put my Spirit within you" (Ezek 36:27). The Pentecost is also a fulfillment of the prophecy of Joel: "And it shall come to pass afterward, that I will pour out my Spirit on all flesh" (Joel 2:28; Acts 2:17). Pentecost is hence the historical moment when Jesus decisively baptized the corporate church with the Spirit to unite her, as a corporate entity, to him. Jesus' baptizing the church with the Spirit is like a marriage ceremony that symbolizes the marital union between Christ and his corporate church.[31] The baptism with the Spirit, to put it differently, is in a corporate sense at Pentecost during which believers of all generations were judicially washed clean in that one baptism.

This unique Pentecostal baptism is expounded by Paul in 1 Cor 12:13, "For in one Spirit we were all baptized into one body [καὶ γὰρ ἐν ἑνὶ πνεύματι ἡμεῖς πάντες εἰς ἓν σῶμα ἐβαπτίσθημεν]—Jews or Greeks, slaves or free—and all were made to drink of one Spirit [πάντες ἓν πνεῦμα ἐποτίσθημεν]." The one Spirit (ἑνὶ πνεύματι) refers to the Holy Spirit. The Spirit, however, is not the initiating agent of this baptism because πνεύματι is not a nominative noun but a dative noun of instrumentality or means.[32] The prepositional phrase ἐν ἑνὶ πνεύματι ("in one Spirit") cannot be taken as an agent because the same phrase ἐν πνεύματι also appears in similar passages in Matt 3:11; Mark 1:8; Luke 3:16; John 1:33; Acts 1:5; and 11:16 in the context of Spirit-baptism. These passages all draw a parallel between John's baptizing with water and Jesus' baptizing with the Spirit. Just as John baptized with water (ἐν ὕδατι), Jesus baptized with Spirit (ἐν πνεύματι). This baptism with the Spirit by Jesus, the unnamed agent in 1 Cor 12:13, occurred, decisively, at Pentecost.

Significantly, Pentecost was an event that happened after Jesus' resurrection and ascension. The church, hence, is not just united to Jesus but to a resurrected and ascended Jesus. Undeniably, only the resurrected and ascended Jesus can give the Spirit to the corporate church. Union with Christ in the corporate sense means that the Spirit who is now in the exalted Christ is

---

30. Technically, the church, consisting of believers from both the old and the new covenants for whom Christ died (Eph 5:25), existed long before Pentecost.

31. One should distinguish between the baptism with the Spirit from the filling with the Spirit. For any believer, the baptism with the Spirit happens only once at regeneration, which is later symbolized by water baptism. This is like a wedding ceremony between the believer and Christ. The filling with the Spirit, in contrast, is like the love between Christ and the individual believer, which believers should experience throughout this spiritual marriage.

32. Wallace, Greek Grammar, 374.

the same Spirit who now indwells the corporate church. Peter expounded on this truth in his sermon at Pentecost: "This Jesus God raised up, and of that we all are witnesses. Being therefore exalted at the right hand of God, and having received from the Father the promise of the Holy Spirit, he has poured out this that you yourselves are seeing and hearing" (Acts 2:32–33). Richard Gaffin points out an instructive parallel between Jesus' baptism and Pentecost:

> At the Jordan, the Spirit was given to Jesus, by the Father (Luke 3:22), as endowment for the messianic task before him, in order that he might accomplish the salvation of the church; in contrast, at Pentecost, the Spirit, was received by Jesus, from the Father, now as reward for the redemptive work finished and behind him, and was given by him to the church as the (promised) gift (of the Father).[33]

Christ is not only the giver of the Spirit but, as the apostle Paul points out in 1 Cor 15:45, "The last Adam became a life-giving Spirit." A oneness exists between the exalted Christ and the Spirit. Gaffin explains, beautifully, the significance of this unity between the ascended Christ and the Spirit:

> The oneness or unity in view is economic or functional, eschatological. Paul's point is that by virtue of his glorification, Christ, as last Adam and second man, has come into such permanent and complete possession of the Spirit that the two are equated in their activity. The two are seen as one, as they have been made one in the eschatological work of giving life to the church.[34] At Pentecost, Christ pours out on the church the gift of the Spirit, but also that Pentecost is the coming to the church of Christ himself as the life-giving Spirit. The Spirit of Pentecost is the resurrection life of Jesus, the life of the exalted Christ, effective in the church.[35] The gift of the Spirit is nothing less than the gift to the church of Christ himself, the glorified Christ who has become what he is by virtue of his sufferings, death and exaltation. In this sense, the giving of the Spirit is the crowning achievement of Christ's work. Pentecost is his coming in exaltation to the church in the power of the Spirit. It completes the once-for-all accomplishment of our salvation. Without it, that work that climaxes in Christ's death and resurrection would be, strictly speaking, unfinished, incomplete.[36]

33. Gaffin, "Holy Spirit," 67.
34. Gaffin, "Holy Spirit," 68.
35. Gaffin, "Holy Spirit," 69.
36. Gaffin, "Holy Spirit," 70.

Pentecost marks the beginning of Jesus' continual ministry on earth through the presence and indwelling of his Spirit in the lives of his people, the church. God's people, consisting of both Jews and gentiles, are "being built together into a dwelling place for God by the Spirit" (Eph 2:22). The indwelling of the Spirit provides the needed *dunamis* (power) for the disciples to be Jesus' witnesses "in Jerusalem and in all Judea and Samaria, and to the end of the earth" (Acts 1:8). The Spirit then takes what is Jesus' and declares it to the believers (John 16:15). Union with Christ is thus ecclesiological because the corporate church is in ecclesiological union with Christ through the indwelling of the Spirit. Moreover, Jesus, through the Spirit, continues to be with the corporate church until the end of the age (Matt 28:20).

F. ASSURANCE AND UNION WITH CHRIST

What is the relationship between assurance and union with Christ? The answer is as simple as it is significant—believers' assurance is rooted in the firm knowledge and confidence that they are in union with Christ. Before believers' justification, they were in union with Adam. Through faith, God translates believers from being in union with Adam to being in union with Christ. Salvation, then, is a by-product or a consequence of being in union with Christ. No one can receive salvation without first being in union with Christ. Therefore, in simple terms, assurance of salvation is assurance of being in union with Christ.

Assurance is not based on a believer's ability to persevere in the Christian faith but on union with Christ, which is the ground upon which God can bless believers with "every spiritual blessing in the heavenly places" (Eph 1:3). These blessings are freely given in Christ to believers through Spirit-engendered faith. One of them is assurance itself, both in the present estate on earth and the next in heaven. As John Murray puts it, regarding any believer, "Why can he have confident assurance with reference to the future and rejoice in hope of the glory of God? It is because he cannot think of past, present, or future apart from union with Christ."[37] He continues to assert that "there is no truth, therefore, more suited to impart confidence and strength, comfort and joy in the Lord than this one of union with Christ."[38]

Since salvation is rooted in union with Christ, it follows that assurance of salvation, as a benefit of salvation itself, is also rooted in this union. Besides, the nature of union with Christ circumscribes the nature of assurance. For instance, since union with Christ is a truth for all believers, assurance,

---

37. Murray, *Redemption Accomplished and Applied*, 164.
38. Murray, *Redemption Accomplished and Applied*, 171.

then, is also a reality for all believers. The degree of assurance varies from person to person and fluctuates for the same person at different life stages and in different circumstances. Still, every believer has some measure of assurance because every believer is in union with Christ. To put it differently, assurance of salvation as an all-encompassing concept, stemming from the manifold riches of salvation, exhibits the characteristics of union with Christ. Since union with Christ has different dimensions—ontological, Christological, pneumatological, historical, experiential, eschatological, already-but-not-yet, and Trinitarian, we shall demonstrate that assurance also shares the characteristics of the union in these same dimensions.

Union with Christ is ontological because it has its basis in the *pactum salutis* within the Godhead. Explicitly, the Father chose some people, the elect, in Christ; the Son would die for them; and the Spirit would apply the redemption earned by Christ to them. Since believers are chosen "in Christ" before creation, through the *pactum salutis*, there is a sense that believers are always "in Christ" or "in union with Christ." Even when these believers, before their justification, were temporarily outside of Christ, in union with Adam, there is a sense they are always ontologically "in Christ" even while they were temporally and temporarily "in Adam."[39] Assurance, in this sense, also has an ontological dimension because it is a benefit of salvation originating from the Father's election in Christ, during which the elect are already ontologically united with Christ through the *pactum salutis*. Assurance of salvation, just like salvation itself, is not an afterthought but is ontologically and eternally rooted in union with Christ.

Union with Christ is Christological because the focus of the union is on the benefactor, Christ, not on the beneficiaries, the elect, much less on the benefits, the graces of salvation. Assurance, in the same vein, is Christological. The primary focus of assurance is looking to Christ in faith—his person, work, and promise—instead of looking introspectively at the lives and fruits of the believers. Since even the holiest of saints still live a life far below the holiness of Christ, believers will severely undermine their assurance if they primarily look to themselves rather than Christ for assurance.

Union with Christ is pneumatological or spiritual because it is the Spirit who applies the riches of the covenant of grace to believers by spiritually uniting them to Christ through faith. Assurance is spiritual as well because it is the Spirit himself who bears witness with believers' spirit that they are children of God (Rom 8:16).

---

39. This apparent paradox of elect being simultaneously in Adam, in one sense, and in Christ, in another, is shared by John Frame, *Systematic Theology*, 914.

Union with Christ is historical and objective, based on the death and resurrection of Jesus. Assurance also has a historical basis as it entails confidence in the historical death and resurrection of Christ, which is the historical foundation of union with Christ. The historical Christian faith is to believe in the Jesus who "was delivered up for our trespasses and raised for our justification" (Rom 4:25). Assurance thus has a firm historical and objective foundation because historical events cannot be changed or reversed.[40]

Union with Christ is experiential as believers can experience this union in their lives. In the process of sanctification, for instance, believers can experience in more considerable measure the fruit of the Spirit. Assurance also has an experiential and subjective dimension based in part on the fruits of sanctification. This sanctification is divinely-enabled due to union with Christ when Christ becomes to believers their sanctification and righteousness (1 Cor 1:30).[41] Even as Christ has resurrected and overcome the dominions of sin and death, so will believers in union with him experience greater deliverance from the power of sin. As believers grow in the richness of their sanctified experience, their assurance will grow accordingly.

Union with Christ is eschatological as believers live in the hope of receiving their resurrected bodies at Christ's return. This union looks forward to the consummation of salvation, which culminates in the messianic banquet between Christ and believers. Assurance also has an eschatological aspect as it is believing in the promise of God that those "whom he predestined he also called, and those whom he called he also justified, and those whom he justified he also glorified" (Rom 8:30). Assurance hinges on trusting that "nothing will separate [believers] from the love of God" (Rom 8:38–39), and one day they will see Christ as he is when he appears (1 John 3:2).

Union with Christ, like so many biblical truths, is "already but not yet." Elect are already in Christ in the *pactum salutis* but, until their justification, they are not yet in union with Christ temporally. Even after their translation from Adam to Christ, they still have not achieved the *telos* of redemption until the consummation of salvation at Christ's return. There is a coexistence of inaugurated and future eschatology. Believers have had a decisive conversion, but they still need to repent and believe daily (1 John 1:9). Believers have been definitively justified by grace through faith (Eph 2:8), but one day they must all appear before the judgment seat of Christ to receive what is due for them (2 Cor 5:10). They are already God's adopted children (Rom 8:15), but they are waiting eagerly for adoption as sons in the redemption

40. God can undoubtedly change the effect and impact of historical events, but not the events themselves.

41. The Greek word translated as "sanctification" is ἁγιασμός, which sometimes is rendered as "holiness."

of their bodies (Rom 8:23) and the full appropriation of their inheritance (1 Pet 1:3–5). They have been definitively sanctified (1 Cor 6:11), but they are continuously growing in the grace and knowledge of Jesus (2 Pet 3:18). They have persevered, but they will continue to persevere until final glorification. They have experienced glorification by being transformed into the image of Christ from one degree of glory to another (2 Cor 3:18), but they also eagerly await the eschatological glorification and bodily resurrection (Phil 3:20–21). For true believers, similarly, assurance is already a reality but not yet fully realized. Believers have assurance by faith, but not yet by sight.[42] Assurance is a present reality because "the Spirit himself bears witness with our spirit that we are children of God" (Rom 8:16), yet, concurrently, it is a goal to be pursued because believers are to make their calling and election sure (2 Pet 1:10). It is, after all, a shared experience for believers to cry out, "I believe; help my unbelief" (Mark 9:24).

Finally, union with Christ is Trinitarian. It is eternally initiated by the Father in the *pactum salutis*, objectively and historically established in the death and resurrection of the Son, and subjectively applied by the Holy Spirit to the elect.[43] Assurance, in a like manner, is Trinitarian but in a reverse order. The Spirit first assures Christians they are children of God because "they have received the Spirit of adoption as sons" by whom they cry, "Abba! Father!" (Rom 8:15–16). They are, consequently, assured they have participated in the death and resurrection of the Son. Only then can they be assured they have been eternally chosen by the Father to be "heirs of God and fellow heirs with Christ" (Rom 8:17). J. Todd Billings tersely spells out this Trinitarian Christian life as one that is "found in Christ, by the Spirit, in service to the Father."[44]

G. IS ASSURANCE OF THE ESSENCE OF FAITH?

Assurance stems from and is rooted in union with Christ. Since no one can be saved apart from being in union with Christ, it follows that for all

---

42. This phrase is taken from the title of Richard Gaffin's book, *By Faith, Not By Sight*. In the book, Gaffin argues that believers have been justified, adopted, sanctified by faith, but not by sight, because they have not been glorified. Nonetheless, he has not included assurance in his treatment of this truth.

43. Richard Gaffin outlines the Trinitarian dimension of union as *predestinarian* (Eph 1:4) in the eternal decrees of God the Father, *redemptive-historical* in the death and resurrection of Jesus, and *existential* when the Spirit applies that union to believers. Gaffin considers these not as three different unions but different aspects of the same union. See Gaffin, *By Faith, Not by Sight*, 42.

44. Billings, *Union with Christ*, 11

who are in union with Christ, they will receive assurance, along with other redemptive benefits. In an objective sense, therefore, assurance is of the essence of faith because everyone who is in Christ will receive it.

In a subjective sense, however, not everyone who is in Christ will feel the same intensity of assurance. It is because assurance spans the whole spectrum of the *ordo salutis*—full assurance entails having confidence one is elected, predestined, effectually called, regenerated, justified, adopted, sanctified, persevering, and will be glorified. Not every believer will have the same knowledge and confidence of these benefits. It is in this sense that assurance, at least full assurance, is not of the essence of faith.

H. SUMMARY

Union with Christ is a theological concept rooted in Scripture. It is the organizing principle of redemptive benefits. It is not one of the benefits of salvation but the fountainhead and basis of all redemptive benefits. At Pentecost, Christ corporately and definitively united the church to him by outpouring his Spirit. Assurance is rooted in union with Christ and takes on the corresponding characteristics. Like union with Christ, assurance is ontological, Christological, pneumatological, historical, experiential, eschatological, already-but-not-yet, and Trinitarian. In the next chapter, we shall study assurance's relationship with the *ordo salutis*, the sacraments, and Pentecost.

Chapter 8

Assurance and the *Ordo Salutis*, the Sacraments, and Pentecost

With the understanding that assurance is a benefit of the *ordo salutis*, which is, comprehensively, union with Christ, this chapter further delineates the relationship between assurance and the *ordo salutis*, the sacraments, and Pentecost. A modified *ordo salutis* will be constructed that takes into account the existential, legal, relational, moral, and eschatological dimensions of salvation.

A. ASSURANCE AND THE *ORDO SALUTIS*

Past and contemporary literature has not explicitly listed assurance as one of the elements in the *ordo salutis*. A possible reason could be that assurance, as confidence that a person is saved and will remain saved forever, is related to the entire spectrum of the *ordo salutis*. A full assurance must entail confidence that believers are elected, predestined, effectually called, regenerated, converted, justified, adopted, sanctified, and are in the process of sanctification and will continue to persevere till glorification. This comprehensive nature of assurance could explain why scholars have not tethered assurance to any element in the *ordo*.

It is a goal of this book to integrate assurance into a proper *ordo salutis*, one that is modified to consider both the inaugurated and future eschatology. To this end, Table 7 shows assurance broken down into its various dimensions—retrospective, historical, definitive, progressive, eschatological, and final.

Table 7: The modified *ordo salutis*

Eternal Past	Past	Past	Past	Present	Future (Death)	Eternal Future (Jesus' Return)
Already	Already	Already	Already	Already, Not Yet	Not Yet	Not Yet
Divine Act	Divine Act	Human Act	Divine Act	Divine-Human Work	Divine Act	Divine Act
Election	Effectual Calling	Conversion	Definitive Justification	Progressive Sanctification	Eschatological Sanctification	Final Justification
Predestination	Regeneration		Definitive Adoption	Progressive Assurance		Final Adoption
			Definitive Sanctification	Perseverance		Final Sanctification
						Glorification
Retrospective Assurance	Historical Assurance	Historical Assurance	Definitive Assurance	Progressive Assurance	Eschatological Assurance	Final Assurance
Assurance of Past Salvation				Assurance of Present Salvation	Assurance of Future Salvation	
Assurance by Faith					Assurance by Faith & Sight	Assurance by Sight

1. The Dimensions of Assurance

The first dimension of assurance, within the framework of the *ordo salutis*, is *retrospective assurance*. It corresponds to believers' assurance they have been elected and predestined from eternity past to receive salvation. Believers are elected in Christ before the foundation of the world to be predestined for adoption as sons through Jesus Christ (Eph 1:4–5). Since election and predestination come from the sovereign action of God in the eternal past, a Christian can only be assured of that fact in the retrospective sense, by looking back in faith on what God has done through the *pactum salutis*. In this sense, a full spectrum of assurance includes not only present confidence of present salvation and present confidence of future salvation but also present confidence of past salvation, rooted in God's election and predestination of the elect in eternity past.

The second dimension of assurance, corresponding to effectual calling, regeneration, and conversion, is *historical assurance*. God, in effectual calling, extends an irresistible call to the elect through the preaching of the gospel. This calling results in regeneration in which the Holy Spirit quickens the elect from spiritually dead to alive by giving the elect new hearts of flesh to replace their hearts of stone (Ezek 36:26). In conversion, which is the fruit of regeneration, the Spirit convicts the elect of sin, righteousness, and judgment unto repentance (John 16:8) to believe in Jesus as Savior and Lord (John 3:16). This supernatural experience constitutes the initial conversion of the elect after being born of the Spirit. Then, throughout the lifetime of the believer, he or she will continue to repent and believe as part of the process of progressive sanctification. Effectual calling and regeneration are purely divine acts, while conversion is a purely human act—it is the sinner, alone, who repents and believes. This assurance is historical because it anchors on the dual historical acts—the divine acts of God in effectual calling and regeneration, and the human act of conversion.

The third dimension is *definitive assurance*, based on definitive justification, definitive adoption, and definitive sanctification. In definitive justification, the righteousness of Christ is imputed to the elect, resulting in the elect's status change before God from guilty to guiltless. The elect's status, in definitive adoption, is changed from sons of wrath in the kingdom of darkness to sons of grace in God's family in the kingdom of light. In definitive sanctification, the elect, having the old man co-crucified with Christ (Rom 6:6), are liberated from being in bondage to sin. This term denotes the initial, decisive, conclusive breach from the power of sin and death by the Spirit, setting the elect apart to serve the living God.[1]

While regeneration is transformative, representing what Christ has done "in us," definitive justification, adoption, and sanctification are forensic in God's court of justice, representing what Christ has done "for us" through his death and resurrection. Nothing is changed internally in the life of the elect in these definitive divine acts.

All elements belonging to historical and definitive assurance are "digital" or "binary" in the sense that they assume either of two values: presence or absence. A person is either effectually called or not, regenerated or not, converted or not, definitively justified or not, definitively adopted or not, and definitively sanctified or not. There is no gradation or middle ground in the status. One believer, to put it differently, cannot be more called, regenerated, converted, definitively justified, definitively adopted, and definitively sanctified than another.

The fourth dimension of assurance, entailing progressive sanctification and perseverance, is *progressive assurance*. Progressive sanctification is not a decisive event but an ongoing process. It involves an ever-increasing

---

1. Definitive sanctification is distinguished from progressive sanctification. A discussion of these two concepts in Scripture is found in Murray, *Collected Writings*, 277–80, 284, 294–96, 299.

degree of denying self and being conformed to the image of Christ. This process is a divine-human *work*, as believers need to put to death the deeds of the flesh by the Spirit (Rom 8:13). It is the same process in which believers, as adopted sons of God, are continuously being "pitied, protected, provided for, and chastened by Him as by a Father."[2] Believers can have different degrees of progressive sanctification. Some believers can bear more fruits than others, in one case a hundredfold, in another sixty, and yet another thirty (Matt 13:23).

Perseverance implies that believers will be steadfast in the faith despite all odds. What sustains believers are the intercessory prayers of Christ (Heb 7:25) and the Spirit (Rom 8:26–27) and the power of God (John 10:29). Perseverance, like progressive sanctification, is capable of degrees. The writer of Hebrews, for example, in five warning passages (Heb 2:1–4; 3:7–4:13; 6:4–8; 10:26–31; 12:25–29),[3] urges the readers to persevere in the Christian faith despite persecutions. As depicted in the dynamic cycle of progressive assurance in Table 7, there is a mutual reinforcement and interplay between progressive sanctification, perseverance, and progressive assurance. Progress in sanctification encourages perseverance, which fosters progressive assurance, which in turn promotes greater sanctification. This concept of positive reinforcement is taught by the apostle Peter when he exhorts believers to "be all the more diligent to confirm your calling and election" (2 Pet 1:10a). One way to confirm the election, Peter notes earlier, is to be diligent in bearing fruits of sanctification (2 Pet 1:5–7) because "if you practice these qualities you will never fall" (2 Pet 1:10b).

The fifth dimension is *eschatological assurance*. At death, a Christian's soul passes into heaven. It is immediately and wholly sanctified to attain to eschatological sanctification. Then, the believer's progressive sanctification will have achieved the level of positional sanctification. The believer, at this stage, is sinless but also bodiless. It is a stage when the assurance of believers is both by faith and by sight. It is by faith in the sense that their salvation is yet to be consummated, which will only occur at Christ's return when they will receive their physical vision from their spiritual bodies. It is by sight as they can already see Christ through their spiritual vision in heaven.

The sixth dimension is *final assurance*. At Christ's second coming, as Paul states in 1 Cor 15:42–43, the believer will receive a spiritual,

---

2. This is the language of WCF chapter 12 on adoption.

3. While scholars agree on the existence of five warning passages in Hebrews, they disagree on where those warnings start or end. My delineation of the first and third to fifth warning passages is based on Guthrie, *Structure of Hebrews*, 135, while the second warning passage is based on Bateman, *Warning Passages in Hebrews*, 27.

imperishable, glorious, and powerful body.[4] This glorification is both discrete and continuous. Regarding the former, a person will either be in the state of eternal glory or damnation. Regarding the latter, believers will experience different degrees of glorification. Paul, in 1 Cor 15:40–42, strongly implies a gradation of glory in believers' resurrected bodies. In a similar vein, both Jesus and Paul teach that there are different degrees of reward in heaven (Luke 19:11–17; Matt 25:14–30; 1 Cor 3:10–15).[5]

The day of Christ's return is also the day when believers will achieve final justification in the sense of being openly acquitted and declared righteous. By receiving the resurrected bodies, believers will also receive the final adoption as sons (Rom 8:23). By possessing resurrected bodies, believers will, at last, achieve final sanctification when not only the soul but the body is wholly sanctified. It is only then that believers' assurance is no longer by faith, but by sight.

In Table 7, some elements are forensic, signifying status change before God, and others are transformative, indicating real changes inside a person's life. The forensic elements include definitive justification, definitive adoption, definitive sanctification, final justification, final adoption, and final sanctification.[6] The transformative elements contain effectual calling, regeneration, conversion, progressive sanctification, and perseverance.

This categorization leaves out eschatological sanctification and glorification, which defy a simple classification as either forensic or transformative. In eschatological sanctification, the person's status changes from "being progressively sanctified" to at once "being fully sanctified." This instant sanctification, however, is not merely a status change but a real change inside the person. Similarly, glorification is not just a status change from "not glorified" to "glorified," because the believer will also receive a spiritual

---

4. By "spiritual" it means that it is created by the Spirit. The body, like Jesus' resurrected body, will still have physical substance.

5. Jonathan Edwards, in his sermon on Romans 2:10 entitled "The Portion of The Righteous," preached in December 1740, said, "There are different degrees of happiness and glory in heaven. As there are degrees among the angels, viz. thrones, dominions, principalities, and powers; so there are degrees among the saints. In heaven are many mansions, and of different degrees of dignity. The glory of the saints above will be in some proportion to their eminency in holiness and good works here." Edwards, *Works of Jonathan Edwards*, 948.

6. In definitive justification, definitive adoption, and definitive sanctification, the person's status is changed, respectively, from guilty to guiltless, from a child of wrath to a child of grace, and from a sinner in bondage to sin to a saint positionally sanctified to serve God. In final justification, final adoption, and final sanctification, by virtue of receiving the resurrected body, the believer's status has achieved final justification, adoption, and sanctification.

body—a real change indeed. Eschatological sanctification and glorification, therefore, are both forensic as well as transformative elements.

The above analysis has excluded election and predestination as they are outside time. It would not be proper to describe them in terms of a status change, for example, from "not being elected" to "elected." It would also not be meaningful to describe them as transformative because God has not even created the elect.

What about assurance? Is it considered as forensic or transformative? To answer that question, one must further ask, "Which assurance?" While definitive assurance has its basis in the objective declaration of God that a person is definitively justified, adopted, and sanctified, progressive assurance is grounded in progressive sanctification and perseverance, which are subjective. Believers not only have different degrees of progressive assurance depending on their varying levels of spiritual growth and maturity, but even for the same believer, the level of progressive assurance can change according to different stages of sanctification and perseverance.

Moreover, since assurance is by faith and faith has both an objective and a subjective ground, assurance itself is both objective and subjective. For these reasons, even as assurance, as least full assurance, encompasses various dimensions—retrospective, historical, definitive, progressive, eschatological, and final, one must conclude that assurance is both forensic and transformative.

2. The Grounds of Assurance

Assurance has many grounds. In the following discussion, we will not consider election, predestination, effectual calling, regeneration, and conversion, as they are preliminary and preparatory elements leading to justification, which is the tipping point of salvation. Believers can be sure they have participated in these graces only by looking at them retrospectively from the vantage point of justification, adoption, sanctification, perseverance, and glorification, which we discussed in the section on WCF 18.2. Therefore, in the following, we will focus on the grounds of assurance of these latter graces.

The first and primary ground of assurance is definitive justification— believers are assured because they are definitively justified. By Christ's resurrection, he is justified in the sense that his righteousness is vindicated, and his innocence maintained (1 Tim 3:16). Sinners can only receive justification through union with the justified Christ. The justification of Christ is the basis of the definitive justification of the sinner. Justification is God's objective declaration that he has forgiven all the sins—past, present, and future—of the sinner.

Justification entails a dual transaction. In the first transaction, the sins of the elect are imputed to Christ, who then died for them in his passive obedience. This vicarious punishment of sins by the Messiah on behalf of his people is deemed complete by Jesus' utterance at the cross, τετέλεσται (it is finished). Jesus' death not only atones for the sins of the elect and expiates their guilt but also propitiates the wrath of God. God vindicates Jesus' innocence and accepts his sacrifice on behalf of the covenant people by raising Jesus from the dead on the third day. In the second transaction, Christ's righteousness, through his active obedience of perfectly keeping all the demands of the law in the covenant of works, is imputed to the elect. It is through these dual transactions—the elect imputing their sins to the Messiah and the Messiah imputing his righteousness to the elect—that elect are definitively justified by grace through faith alone. This faith is not inherent in the elect but is a fruit of regeneration and a gift of God: "For by grace you have been saved through faith. And this is not your own doing; it is the gift of God" (Eph 2:8).

Justification, therefore, is Trinitarian as it is an objective act of God the Father declaring the elect as righteous, based on the historical death and resurrection of the Son, and effected by the Spirit in uniting the elect to Christ through faith. The most objective ground of assurance, hence, is to believe in the promises of God that he justifies sinners who put their trust in Christ as their Savior and Lord (John 3:16; Rom 4:5).

The second ground of assurance is definitive adoption—believers are assured because they are definitively adopted. Adoption is God's act of receiving the elect as his adopted sons. The apostle Paul speaks of Jesus' adoption in Rom 1:4: "He was declared to be the Son of God in power according to the Spirit of holiness by his resurrection from the dead."

Definitive adoption follows from definitive justification because only the justified Son can justify the sons in Adam to make them the "sons in the Son,"[7] by way of their union with the adopted Son through faith. Paul says in Gal 3:26, "For in Christ Jesus you are all sons of God, through faith." These sons of God are those who "were baptized into Christ" (Gal 3:27). The ground of adoption, therefore, is "in Christ" by being "baptized into Christ" through faith, which is the same instrumental means as definitive justification. Believers, through union with Christ, are adopted sons of God and enjoy all the filial benefits as sons in God's family. The pivotal passage is Rom 8:14–16: "For all who are led by the Spirit of God are sons of God. For

---

7. This is taken from the title of the seminal book by Garner, *Sons in the Son*.

you did not receive the spirit of slavery to fall back into fear, but *you have received the Spirit of adoption as sons,* by whom we cry, 'Abba! Father!' The Spirit himself bears witness with our spirit that we are children of God." As argued in chapter 2, an adoption-centric understanding of assurance most comprehensively captures the theological richness of salvation.

The third ground of assurance is definitive sanctification—believers are assured because they are definitively sanctified. In the general sense, sanctification is the work of the Holy Spirit in the lives of the redeemed to conform them to the likeness of Jesus Christ, who, by his resurrection, is himself sanctified in the sense that he died to sins once and lives to God forever (Rom 6:10). Sinners can only experience sanctification through their Spirit-engendered union with the sanctified Christ. The sanctification of Christ is the ground for the sanctification of sinners.

The New Testament speaks of sanctification in five ways. First, it is a definitive and accomplished act in Christ. Paul addresses the believers in the Corinthian church as "those *sanctified* in Christ Jesus, called to be saints" (1 Cor 1:2). The word "sanctified" is ἡγιασμένοις, which is a passive perfect participle signifying an action already happened in the past but has an ongoing effect. Speaking to the Corinthians, Paul says, "You *were washed,* you *were sanctified,* you *were justified*" (1 Cor 6:11). All three verbs are aorist indicative, denoting completed actions, already happened in the past. Here, "you were washed" refers to regeneration. Of significance is the sequence of putting sanctification, that is, definitive sanctification, before justification. This reversal in order comes from the fact that definitive sanctification is a finished act, so the Corinthians "were sanctified" just as they "were justified." Definitive sanctification is rooted in believers' union with Christ in his historical death, burial, and resurrection, as expounded by Paul in Rom 6:1–11.

Because of definitive sanctification, believers also have positional sanctification, which is the believers' new sanctified status before God. In Paul's letters to the seven churches, he addresses the readers most frequently as "saints" (Rom 1:7; 1 Cor 1:2; 2 Cor 1:1; Eph 1:1; Phil 1:1; Col 1:2).[8] Paul, therefore, can call the Corinthians, as spiritually immature as they were (1 Cor 3:1–4), saints. They were, in their sanctified position, set apart as holy even though many of them were still infants in Christ. This title of "saints" is in stark contrast to their old title of "sinners." The new title speaks of the reality that believers, having been definitively sanctified, are now being set apart to serve God alone. Definitive and positional sanctification is the

8. The only two exceptions are the churches in Galatia and Thessalonica, where Paul simply addresses the recipients as "church" (Gal 1:2; 1 Thess 1:1; 2 Thess 1:1). Nevertheless, the word "church" refers to none other than those who are called out of the world to be "saints."

foundation upon which believers can experience progressive sanctification throughout life.

As is well known, sanctification also has a progressive sense, as expounded in Rom 6:12–23. Believers, says Paul in 2 Cor 3:18, are "being transformed into the same image [of Christ] from one degree of glory to another." Progressive sanctification is made plain in Peter's exhortation to believers to successively add to the Christian faith with virtue, knowledge, self-control, steadfastness, godliness, brotherly affection, and, finally, love (2 Pet 1:5–7). As sanctification grows, assurance grows with it.

At death, believers experience eschatological sanctification in the soul when God purges all vestiges of sinfulness. Believers will experience instant transformation into holiness. Indeed, without holiness, no one will see the Lord (Heb 12:14).

Lastly, at Christ's second coming, believers will experience final sanctification when their bodies are resurrected imperishable, in holiness, glory, and power (1 Cor 15:42–43). In sum, believers are assured because they have been, are being, and will be sanctified.

The fourth ground of assurance is perseverance—believers are assured because they are persevering. God's preservation, which is upheld by both Christ and the Father (John 10:28–29), ensures believers' perseverance. This preservation guarantees that once God has joined believers to Christ through faith, no one can snatch them out of the hands of the Father and the Son. Nothing will be able to separate believers from the love of God (Rom 8:38–39). Preservation comes from God's effort: "It is God who establishes [βεβαιῶν] us with you in Christ, and has anointed us" (2 Cor 1:21). The present active nominative participle βεβαιῶν translates to "stands firm" in NIV. It is thus God's ongoing and sovereign action to cause believers to stand firm in their faith till the end. God's preservation underlies the perseverance of the saints.[9] This dual truth of preservation and perseverance is joined together in Phil 2:12–13: "Work out your own salvation with fear and trembling, for it is God who works in you, both to will and to work for his good pleasure." As illustrated in Table 7, there is a positive feedback loop among perseverance, progressive assurance, and progressive sanctification. They feed on each other positively in a growing and reinforcing cycle.

The fifth ground of assurance is glorification. Believers, through union with the glorified Christ, are also glorified as they are continuously being transformed into the image of the Son from one degree of glory to another

---

9. John Murray prefers the phrase "perseverance of the saints" to "eternal security" in order to guard against the mentality that a Christian is "secure as to his eternal salvation quite irrespective of the extent to which he may fall into sin and backslide from faith and holiness." Murray, *Redemption Accomplished and Applied*, 154.

(2 Cor 3:18). Perseverance and glorification are distinct yet inseparable, representing, respectively, the present and future aspects of salvation. Perseverance guarantees and leads to glorification, which is the consummation and climax of believers' salvation. The *telos* of salvation materializes at glorification—believers are, finally, body and soul, united with Christ—to the praise of God's glory.

Speaking of glorification, Marcus Johnson puts it beautifully:

> In this glorious work, God's creation purpose, "Let us make man in our image" (Gen 1:26), converges with his re-creative purpose, "those whom he foreknew he also predestined to be conformed to the image of his Son" (Rom 8:29). We will be the image of God again, fully, perfectly, and finally the image of God in Christ. . . . Glorification, then, can be defined as the final, complete, and eternal enjoyment of perfect union with Christ, through which all the benefits of his person and work are fully, completely, and eternally realized in us, and by which we experience blessed fellowship with God forever.[10]

Glorification marks the occasion when all the redemptive benefits believers have received from Christ through their union with him will be consummated and complete. Believers' assurance, then, consists of persevering unto final glorification.

While believers can view assurance from these redemptive benefits—justification, adoption, sanctification, perseverance, and glorification—stemming from union with the justified, adopted, sanctified, persevered, and glorified Christ, adoption is the highest and most comprehensive benefit encompassing the existential, judicial, relational, moral, and eschatological dimensions of salvation. As such, an adoption-centric understanding of assurance most comprehensively captures the theological richness of salvation.

B. ASSURANCE AND THE SACRAMENTS

Both baptism and communion have rich meanings. They are the signs and seals of the new covenant. The former is a definitive sign signifying entrance into the covenant of grace, and the latter is an ongoing sign representing continuance in the same. The corresponding Old Testament rites are circumcision and Passover meals. Union with Christ is sacramental because it is through the sacraments of the baptism and the Lord's Supper that

---

10. Johnson, *One with Christ*, 182.

believers, in a sacramental sense through the elements of water, bread, and wine, are united to Christ.

Baptism is the initial rite of participation in the covenant of grace and the visible church. Jesus officially commands baptism in the Great Commission—"baptizing them in the name (εἰς τὸ ὄνομα) of the Father, Son, and the Holy Spirit" (Matt 28:19). The use of εἰς (into) instead of ἐν (in), according to Lars Hartman, reflects the Semitic *leshem* formula and is intended to distinguish a Trinity-specific baptism from other baptisms.[11] The use of the singular name, τὸ ὄνομα, referring to the Father, Son, and the Holy Spirit as a composite entity, essentially indicates a union not merely with Jesus in baptism but the fullness of the Godhead.

Peter, in his sermon preached at Pentecost, urged the new converts to be baptized in the name of Jesus Christ only (Acts 2:38). In the Old Testament, whenever God changed a person's name, it denotes the beginning of a new and more intimate relationship between the person and God.[12] Being baptized into Jesus' name signifies being united to him and in union with him. Since Jesus is in union with both the Father and the Spirit in ontological Trinity, union with Christ translates to union with the other members of the Trinity as well. Baptism, Paul teaches in Rom 6:1–11, is a symbol of believers' union with Christ in his death, burial, and resurrection. Baptism is thus a one-time visible sign signifying the unrepeatable nature of union with Christ.

Baptism is a rite that symbolizes God's singular work for the sinner to be regenerated, justified, adopted, and sanctified. Due to the original sin of Adam, the sinner is dead spiritually in Adam's death. God undoes it by quickening the soul of the sinner to life (Titus 3:5). The sinner also inherits the legal guilt of Adam, their representative head (Rom 5:12, 19; 1 Cor 15:22a). God undoes this by definitive justification, which is to declare, legally, that the sinner is now righteous through the imputation of Christ's righteousness to the sinner. Due to sin, the sinner has also become estranged from God and becomes, by nature, a child of wrath (Eph 2:3). God undoes it by reconciling the sinner to him through definitive adoption, admitting the sinner into his family, and restoring the once hostile relationship into one of fatherly love. Furthermore, the sinner also inherits the sinful nature of Adam, which corrupts the image and likeness of God in the sinner (Rom 3:23). God undoes it by breaking the power and enslavement of sin through definitive sanctification. In brief, the decisive act of baptism symbolizes the

---

11. Hartman, "Baptize," 432.

12. For instance, God changed the name of Abram to Abraham (Gen 17:5). God also changed the name of Abraham's grandson from Jacob to Israel (Gen 32:28).

decisive, once-for-all union with Christ that the sinner has definitively been regenerated, justified, adopted, and sanctified.

The Lord's Supper, on the other hand, is an ongoing rite of the participation in the covenant of grace and the visible church. In Jesus' self-identification as the bread of life from heaven, he says, "Unless you eat the flesh of the Son of Man and drink his blood, you have no life in you" (John 6:53). The Lord's Supper vividly depicts the meaning of that statement when believers eat the bread and drink the cup. That action symbolizes, in the spiritual sense, eating Jesus' flesh and drinking his blood, which signifies the nourishing of believers' spiritual life.

The significance of the Lord's Supper is thus a continuous union with Christ, ingesting the very flesh and blood of Christ in the spiritual sense into the lives of the believers to sustain and grow their spiritual lives. Furthermore, when Paul says, "For as often as you eat this bread and drink the cup," this points to perseverance in the faith. When he says, "You proclaim the Lord's death until he comes," this refers to believers' future glorification. More specifically, the content of the Lord's Supper signifies progressive sanctification, its continual observance conveys perseverance, and its final observance (before death) points to glorification.

Assurance is sacramental because Paul teaches in 1 Cor 12:13 that all believers were baptized into one body and drank of one Spirit. The first half of the verse is portrayed by water baptism, the second half by the Lord's Supper. In this way, a believer's assurance is initially confirmed in baptism and receives ongoing strengthening as he or she drinks of the Spirit in the Lord's Supper.

By the two sacraments of baptism and the Lord's Supper, therefore, Jesus has taught believers all the essential elements of the *ordo salutis*—regeneration, justification, adoption, sanctification, perseverance, and glorification—in a visual sermon. A believer's assurance is, consequently, strengthened through participation in the sacraments.

Through the act of water baptism, believers obtain assurance Christ died and was raised "*for* them," and they have died and risen "*with* him." Through the Lord's Supper, believers garner the confidence that Christ is now living "*in* them," and they are also "*in* Christ." Table 8 illustrates the symbolic connection between assurance and the sacraments.

Table 8: The symbolic connection between assurance and the sacraments.

Effectual Calling	Conversion	Definitive Justification	Progressive Sanctification	Eschatological Sanctification	Final Justification
Regeneration		Definitive Adoption	Progressive Assurance		Final Adoption
		Definitive Sanctification	Perseverance		Final Sanctification
					Glorification
Historical Assurance	Historical Assurance	Definitive Assurance	Progressive Assurance	Eschatological Assurance	Final Assurance
Symbolized by Baptism			Symbolized by the Lord's Supper		
Manifests Union with Christ			Manifests Communion with Christ		

C. ASSURANCE AND PENTECOST

Pentecost marks the transition between the work of the Spirit in the old covenant to the new covenant. At Pentecost, the Spirit of Christ indwelled the corporate church. This corporate indwelling is distinguished from the individual indwelling of the Spirit of Christ in the believer to unite him or her to Christ through faith during regeneration (John 3:3–8; Ezek 36:25–27). Pentecost's significance is such that the fullness of the Spirit in Christ is now also in the corporate church, the body of Christ. What indwells the head now also indwells the body. The believer, at regeneration, was individually baptized by Jesus, with the Spirit, to join the universal church, which was baptized by Jesus at Pentecost. In a real sense, this individual baptism by the Spirit is, for the believer, a *personal* Pentecost.

The two baptisms, the corporate baptism of the church and the individual baptism of the believer, though separated by time, are logically and spiritually one single event by having the same baptizer, Christ, and the same instrumentality of baptism, the Spirit. The baptism of the corporate church at Pentecost, in turn, unites the church to Jesus' death and resurrection. This corporate baptism existentially cleansed the church, judicially justified the church, relationally adopted the church, and morally sanctified the church, all decisively and definitively, as his witness and representation on earth.

As believers ponder their salvation, not only are they personally identified with Christ, but they are also corporately united to Christ—the ideal of "I will be your God, and you will be my people" is actualized. A correct understanding of these truths of Pentecost, both personal and corporate, will enhance the assurance of believers.

D. IS ASSURANCE OF THE ESSENCE OF FAITH?

This question is not as simple as it first appears because, as argued in this chapter, there are different dimensions of assurance—retrospective assurance, historical assurance, definitive assurance, progressive assurance, eschatological assurance, and final assurance. A Christian may fully possess one aspect of assurance but wholly lack another. A Wesleyan believer, for instance, might have a robust historical assurance he or she has been born again, but no eschatological or final assurance. Another believer, fully convinced of the dogma "once saved, always saved," might have full final assurance but only partial progressive assurance. The nature of both assurance and faith needs to be further clarified to answer the question. Nevertheless, an adoption-centric understanding of assurance, as argued in this book, will bring clarity to the question at hand.

E. SUMMARY

Assurance is a redemptive benefit derived from union with Christ. From the vantage point of systematic theology, assurance is multifaceted. It entails retrospective assurance, historical assurance, definitive assurance, progressive assurance, eschatological assurance, and final assurance. We have incorporated these concepts into a modified *ordo salutis* that reflects both the inaugurated and future eschatology in Reformed theology. The sacraments enhance assurance because baptism and the Lord's Supper visually manifest union and communion with Christ. When the sacraments are correctly understood and administered, they can enhance believers' assurance. In simple terms that best capture the rich meaning of salvation, assurance is a confidence one is an adopted child of God now and forever. In Part V, we shall briefly explore the pastoral implications of an adoption-centric understanding of assurance.

PART V

Pastoral Implications and Conclusion

Chapter 9

Pastoral Implications

Doubt on assurance is a universal experience for Christians. The good news is that the Scripture has already prescribed the cure. When the Philippian jailer asked Paul and Silas, "Sirs, what must I do to be saved?" Paul unequivocally replied, "Believe in the Lord Jesus, and you will be saved, you and your household (Acts 16:29–31)." As Peter proclaims, "For there is no other name under heaven given among men by which we must be saved (Acts 4:12)." Jesus himself says, "Whoever believes in him should not perish but have eternal life" (John 3:16). In principle, if believers fully heed and believe these words, they will know, by looking to God in faith and trusting his promises in Scripture, that they are saved. Still, in reality, scores of believers at one point or another, even seasoned ones, do not have assurance. How should a pastor counsel those parishioners who are struggling with their assurance? This chapter endeavors to answer this question.

A. PASTORAL COUNSEL ON ASSURANCE

To counsel believers struggling with assurance, the pastor must teach them that the only sure foundation of assurance is faith in the finished work of Christ and God's promise that whosoever believes in his son has eternal life. What is the core promise of the gospel? "These are written," as the apostle John writes in John 20:31, "so that you may believe that Jesus is the Christ, the Son of God, and that by believing you may have life in his name."

Genuine assurance cannot rise above genuine faith. Therefore, a valid assurance presupposes a valid faith. What does this faith entail?

Based on John 20:31, saving faith has an object—Jesus. The name Jesus, meaning "Savior," speaks of his humanity and the redemptive work he came to accomplish, which is to save his people from their sins (Matt 1:21). Moreover, this Jesus is the Christ, meaning the "anointed one." As the anointed one, he is simultaneously the prophet, priest, and king, as only these three offices, the Old Testament teaches us, require God's anointing. However, this Jesus, the Christ, is also the Son of God. He is no mere human. He is also God in the fullest sense of the word. True faith, as such, consists of believing in the humanity, deity, office, and the mission of Jesus. In other words, the content of faith entails the nature, person, and works of Jesus.

Believing in the right content, however, is necessary but not sufficient. People must also personally embrace Jesus, not merely believing in some facts, however orthodox, about Jesus. Paul's answer to the jailer is not "believe in the works of Jesus," not even "believe in the words of Jesus," but "believe in the Lord Jesus." People, in other words, must embrace Jesus as Lord. They need to establish a personal, subjective, experiential relationship with Jesus. Furthermore, this faith is not a one-time event, as if people merely decided on a crusade to come forward to receive Jesus. This faith in Jesus as their personal Lord is ongoing, judging from the present active participle "believing" in John 20:31. It is only by "believing" (πιστευοντες) that people may have life in his name.

Believers' assurance, therefore, does not come through faith in their faith, but faith in the gospel promise of God founded on the redemption accomplished by Christ's death and resurrection. This faith, at its heart, is a continuous embracing of Jesus as Lord. If a pastor consistently teaches the truth about real belief, then people's faith, and by extension assurance, will be founded on solid ground.

Other than building on a biblical foundation of true belief, assurance can hardly increase if there is not a corresponding increase in holiness. There is thus a role for sanctification or good works in promoting assurance. Q. 86 of the HC addresses this very issue:

Q. 86: Since we have been delivered from our misery by grace alone through Christ, without any merit of our own, why must we yet do good works?

A. 86: Because Christ, having redeemed us by His blood, also renews us by His Holy Spirit to be His image, so that with our whole life we may show ourselves thankful to God for His benefits,[1] and He may be praised by us.[2] Further, that *we ourselves may be assured of our faith by its fruits,*[3] and that by our godly walk of life we may win our neighbors for Christ.[4]1

One component of assurance, states A. 86, comes from the fruits in the lives of the believers. Since a believer's fruit varies, assurance also varies accordingly. Hence, as significant as sanctification is, the evidence of sanctification can only serve as a supplementary and not a primary basis of assurance.

The answer to Q. 86 points to the subjective aspect of assurance. This subjectivity does not mean that assurance comes from the feeling or religious experience of the believers, but on the changed life, the fruits, of them.[2] Good works, WCF 16.2 also teaches, can strengthen assurance: "These good works, done in obedience to God's commandments, are the fruits and evidences of a true and lively faith: and by them believers manifest their thankfulness, *strengthen their assurance. . . .*"

What, exactly, are some of these good works? After surveying the Puritan Anthony Burgess's *magnum opus* on conversion and assurance, *Spiritual Refining*, Joel Beeke summarizes examples of some true and false signs of grace, based on Burgess's sermons on assurance:

> True signs include obedience, sincerity, opposition against and abstinence from sin, openness to divine examination, growth in grace, spiritual performance of duties, and love to the godly. Signs that fall short of saving grace include outward church privileges; spiritual gifts; affections of the heart in holy things; judgments and opinions about spiritual truth; great sufferings for Christ; strictness in religion; zeal in false worship; external obedience to the law of God; belief in the truths of religion; a peaceable frame of heart and persuasion of God's love; outward success; prosperity and greatness in the world; and abandonment of gross sins.[3]

The list is undoubtedly helpful as a guide, yet a mature believer must be able to differentiate between the object of faith and its intensity. Richard Philips says it well: "While our strongest faith is unable to save us (i.e., if it was on the wrong object), the weakest faith in Christ grasps a mighty Savior in whom we may rest our souls."[4] Similarly, John Rogers (1570–1636),

1. [1] Rom 6:13; 12:1–2; 1 Pet 2:5–10. [2] Matt 5:16; 1 Cor 6:19–20. [3] Matt 7:17–18; Gal 5:22–24; 2 Pet 1:10–11. [4] Matt 5:14–16; Rom 14:17–19; 1 Pet 2:12; 3:1–2.

2. Clark, *Recovering the Reformed Confession*, 113–15.

3. Beeke, "Assurance Debate," 275–76, quoting from Burgess, *Spiritual Refining*, 61–200.

4. Phillips, "Assured in Christ," 84.

the English Puritan preacher, says, "Neither are we saved by the worth or quantity of our Faith, but by Christ, which is laid hold on by a weak Faith, as well as a strong."[5]

Since assurance depends in part on fruits of sanctification, believers must avail themselves of the means of grace, which will foster growth in the fruits of the believers. What are those means of grace? The WSC provides a concise description in Q. and A. 88:

> Q. 88: What are the outward and ordinary means whereby Christ communicateth to us the benefits of redemption?

> A. 88: The outward and ordinary means whereby Christ communicateth to us the benefits of redemption are, his ordinances, especially the Word, sacraments, and prayer; all which are made effectual to the elect for salvation.[6]

Here, the Westminster Standards once again offer rich teaching regarding how these means of grace can be the means of spiritual growth for believers.[7] The three primary means of grace are Scripture, sacraments, and prayer. For instance, in terms of utilizing Scripture, the pastor can read to those who are struggling with assurance Hebrews 10:19–25:

> *10:19* Therefore, brothers, since we have confidence to enter the holy places by the blood of Jesus, *20* by the new and living way that he opened for us through the curtain, that is, through his flesh, *21* and since we have a great priest over the house of God, *22 let us draw near with a true heart in full assurance of faith,* with our hearts sprinkled clean from an evil conscience and our bodies washed with pure water. *23 Let us hold fast the confession of our hope without wavering,* for he who promised is faithful. *24* And let us consider how to *stir up one another to love and good works, 25* not neglecting to meet together, as is the habit of some, but encouraging one another, and all the more as you see the Day drawing near.

This beautiful passage speaks of the historical aspect of assurance based on Jesus' atonement (vv. 19–21), the present aspects of assurance based on the theological virtues of faith (v. 22), hope (v. 23), love (v. 24), and the means

---

5. Rogers, *Doctrine of Faith*, 201.

6. Matt 28:18–20; Acts 2:41–42.

7. Regarding the word as a means of grace, it is addressed in WLC A. 155. For sacraments as a means of grace, it is covered in WLC A. 161, 162. For prayers as a means of grace, it is described in WSC A. 98.

of grace through which believers' assurance can continue to flourish into the future (v. 25).

For the sacraments, the pastor needs to make baptismal service an occasion of celebration and teaching. The whole church should attend and come together not only to rejoice with the newly baptized but also to learn the meaning and significance of baptism anew. After all, baptism is simultaneously a covenantal sign of entering the covenant of grace, a soteriological sign of union with Christ, a redemptive sign of receiving the benefits of redemption, an ecclesiastical sign of joining the body of Christ, and an eschatological sign of anticipating the marriage union between Christ and the church. Furthermore, the baptismal sermon, action (sprinkling or immersion), and testimony all work to strengthen the faith and assurance of those believers who attend the ordinance.

Likewise, each occasion of the Lord's Supper is not only a commemoration and celebration of what Christ has done on the cross but also a teaching moment. Through the elements of the bread and the cup, the pastor can teach the profound truth of not only union with Christ but also communion with him.

Prayer is the third means of grace mentioned in WSC A. 88. Indeed, as Rom 8:15–16 teaches, assurance of adoption, and thus assurance of salvation, is imparted in the context of prayers. The pastor should not only encourage believers to pray to God and with one another, but the pastor should pray with them regularly if possible.

There can be other means of grace in addition to the traditional triad of word, sacraments, and prayer found in Reformed theology. For instance, Wayne Grudem, in his broad conception of the means of grace, also includes worship, church discipline, giving, spiritual gifts, fellowship, evangelism, and personal ministry to individuals.[8]

When believers have grasped the centrality of the objective promises of God in Christ for salvation, the importance of cultivating the fruit of the Spirit, and the utility of the means of grace, they can expect the Holy Spirit will witness with their spirits that they are children of God. To put it differently, they will receive assurance of adoption and thus assurance of salvation.

B. ADOPTION-CENTRIC ASSURANCE

How does an adoption-centric understanding of assurance help those who are struggling with assurance? Primarily, it helps to orient believers to view

8. Grudem, *Systematic Theology*, 950–51.

their relationship with God in a familial light. Succinctly, assurance of adoption is secure because the Heavenly Father will not disown or disinherit his adopted children, even if they were disobedient at times. God would chastise believers as a loving father would his children (Heb 12:5–11), but he would not cast his children out of the family of God.

In traditional theological conception, Christians view God as their Creator and Sustainer, Jesus as their Savior and Lord, the Spirit as their Revealer and Guider, and people who are saved by the Triune God as the redeemed of God. All these are undoubtedly true, but an adoption-centric understanding of assurance enhances believers' grasp of salvation and assurance. It enables believers to view salvation in the most intimate, familial, filial terms, with the warmest affection.

Under the rubric of adoption, believers view God as their Father and Provider, Jesus as their Elder Brother (Heb 2:11–12), the Spirit as the Spirit of adoption, and other Christians as their brothers and sisters in this family of God. Furthermore, as God's children, they are waiting for their inheritance. The Spirit is the guarantee, the earnest, and the pledge of their inheritance until they possess it (Eph 1:14). This filial view of God as Father provides tremendous comfort to those who need it most.

A pastor can help the parishioners struggling with assurance by pointing out the truths contained in the fivefold use of adoption by Paul. When believers doubt their salvation, they should consider that God has predestined believers for adoption as sons through Jesus Christ (Eph 1:5). Since God authors adoption before the foundation of the world, no one can alter that authorship as no one else, other than God, is present before creation. This truth, when understood correctly, enables those in doubt to shift the focus away from themselves towards God.

Moreover, since the Old Testament period anticipates adoption (Rom 9:4), this demonstrates God's purpose of ever desiring to be the God and Father of his people. Those in doubt should realize that God wants to draw near to believers as a father to his sons. This knowledge will help those in doubt, very often due to a sense of unworthiness, to approach God boldly, knowing the Father will not drive away his sons when they come in brokenness and faith to him.

Adoption is also realized with the arrival of God's Son, Jesus Christ, to redeem those who were under the law, so that they might receive adoption as sons (Gal 4:5). Those in doubt are encouraged to look to Christ, God's only Son, who died, rose, ascended, and is seated at the right hand of God to become believers' Elder Brother. Looking to Jesus strengthens assurance because it underscores what Christ has done as the basis for believers' son-ship, not what they have done or are doing for themselves. Everett Harrison says it well:

> All too often a believer may come to the point of doubting his salvation because his sanctification has proceeded so slowly and so lamely. The Spirit, however, does not base his assuring testi-mony on the progress or the lack of it in the Christian life. He does not lead us to cry, "I am God's child." Rather, he leads us to call upon God as Father, to look away from ourselves to him who established the relationship.[9]

Adoption is also assured by the Spirit who testifies with believers' spirit that they are children of God (Rom 8:16). Those in doubt can be confident their adoption is real precisely in their suffering with Christ, knowing one day they will be glorified with him (Rom 8:17). This assurance through suf-fering can be compelling as Jesus, in the climax of the Beatitudes, proclaims, "Blessed are those who are persecuted for righteousness' sake, for theirs is the kingdom of heaven" (Matt 5:10).

Lastly, adoption also entails a sure hope one day believers will receive their final adoption as sons, the redemption of their bodies (Rom 8:23). This eschatological hope again encourages those in doubt to fix their eyes on the future when their salvation is complete. As a result, they can perceive their present weaknesses or failures in a proper perspective and look forward to the day of final redemption.

This adoption-centric understanding of assurance is rooted in union with Christ, not merely a union with his works. When believers possess Christ, they also possess everything in Christ—not just the privileges and glory, but also duty and suffering. It is precisely when believers collectively cry out "Abba! Father!" that their assurance of adoption is confirmed. As adopted children of God, they can be sure one day their assurance is no longer by faith, but by sight.

9. Harrison, "Romans," 93.

Chapter 10

Conclusion

This book has proposed a new paradigm for understanding the assurance of salvation. It has argued that an adoption-centric understanding of assurance, based on union with Christ, most comprehensively captures the theological richness of salvation.

We have traced the fivefold usage of υἱοθεσία by the apostle Paul—the authoring (Eph 1:5), anticipation (Rom 9:4), arrival (Gal 4:4–5), assurance (Rom 8:15), and achievement (Rom 8:23) of adoption—to demonstrate the significance of adoption in redemptive history, from past to future eternity.

We have studied assurance from different perspectives. From the angle of historical theology, this study has surveyed the views of a few influential theologians and considered the differences between the Heidelberg Catechism and the Westminster Confession of Faith on assurance.

From the perspective of exegetical and biblical theology, we have analyzed assurance in Rom 8:12–17 and the First Epistle of John. The apostle Paul's view on assurance is adoption-centric. He considers assurance as a ministry of the Holy Spirit who testifies with the spirit of believers, in their cry of "Abba, Father," that they are children of God. The apostle John, in contrast, adopts a notion of assurance that is regeneration-centric, sanctification-centric, and perseverance-centric.

From the perspective of systematic theology, we have examined assurance's relationship with union with Christ, the *ordo salutis*, the sacraments, and Pentecost. We have created a modified *ordo salutis* that takes into account the existential, legal, relational, moral, and eschatological dimensions of both assurance and salvation and their dynamic relationships.

We have shown that while assurance of a general nature should accompany true believers, a full measure of infallible assurance at every moment of life is not essential to faith. Assurance, in other words, is of the wellbeing of faith, not the being of it.

Understanding assurance of adoption as assurance of salvation fosters assurance itself. It helps believers to see that God desires not only to have a people for his kingdom but children in his family. This filial intimacy that comes with adoption further helps believers to be assured of their salvation because they are confident of their status as God's adopted children.

We have come a long way in our quest for assurance of adoption. Sometimes God assures his children that they are his in a special way. On the very day that my father passed away in late 2019, I received an email from the publisher that my book proposal on assurance of adoption was accepted for publication. It was a day when different emotions strangely mingled. I was comforted that even as my earthly father has left me, I was not an orphan but an adopted child of my Heavenly Father who would never leave me nor forsake me, especially when I cried out to him, "Abba! Father!" On that day or any other day, this assurance of adoption is not merely historical, exegetical, or theological, but personal to the core. Indeed, God would desire each of his children to come to experience this assurance of adoption when "the Spirit bears witness with our spirit that we are children of God."

Bibliography

Aquinas, Thomas. *Summa Theologiae*. Translated by Cornelius Ernst. Oxford: Blackfriars, 1971.

Barrett, C. K. *The Epistles to the Romans*. Black's New Testament Commentary. 2nd ed. London: A & C Black, 1991.

Barrett, Lee C., III. *The Heidelberg Catechism: A New Translation for the Twenty-First Century*. Cleveland: Pilgrim, 2007.

Bass, Christopher D. *That You May Know: Assurance of Salvation in 1 John*. Nashville: B & H, 2008.

Bateman, Herbert W., IV. *Four Views on the Warning Passages in Hebrews*. Grand Rapids: Kregel, 2007.

Bavinck, Herman. *The Certainty of Faith*. St. Catharines, ON: Paideia, 1980.

Beale, Greg K. *A New Testament Biblical Theology*. Grand Rapids: Baker, 2011.

Beasley-Murray, George R. *John*. Word Biblical Commentary 36. 2nd ed. Dallas: Word, 2002.

Beeke, Joel R. "The Assurance Debate: Six Key Questions." In *Drawn into Controversie: Reformed Theological Diversity and Debates within Seventeenth-Century British Puritanism*, edited by Michael A. G. Haykin and Mark Jones, 263–83. Oakville, CT: Vandenhoeck & Ruprecht, 2011.

———. *Assurance of Faith: Calvin, English Puritanism, and the Dutch Second Reformation*. New York: Peter Lang, 1991.

———. "Does Assurance Belong to the Essence of Faith? Calvin and the Calvinists." *Master's Seminary Journal* 5.1 (1994) 43–71.

———. "Faith and Assurance in the Heidelberg Catechism and Its Primary Composers: A Fresh Look at the Kendall Thesis." *Calvin Theological Journal* 27.1 (1992) 39–67.

———. *Heirs with Christ: The Puritans on Adoption*. Grand Rapids: Reformation Heritage, 2008.

———. "Is Assurance of the Essence of Faith? Calvin and the Calvinists." Paper presented at the 41st National Conference of Evangelical Theological Society, San Diego, CA, November 16–18, 1989.

———. *Living for God's Glory: An Introduction to Calvinism*. Lake Mary, FL: Reformation Trust, 2008.

———. *Knowing and Growing in Assurance of Faith*. Fearn, UK: Christian Focus, 2017.

————. "Personal Assurance of Faith: The Puritans and Chapter 18.2 of the Westminster Confession." *Westminster Theological Journal* 55.1 (1993) 1–30.

————. *Quest for Full Assurance: Legacy of Calvin and His Successors*. Edinburgh: Banner of Truth, 1999.

Beeke, Joel R., and Sinclair B. Ferguson. *Reformed Confessions Harmonized*. Grand Rapids: Baker, 1999.

Bell, M. Charles. *Calvin and Scottish Theology: The Doctrine of Assurance*. Edinburgh: Handsel, 1985.

Berkhof, Louis. *The Assurance of Faith*. Grand Rapids: Eerdmans, 1939.

————. *Systematic Theology*. Louisville, KY: GLH, 2017.

Bierma, Lyle D. *An Introduction to the Heidelberg Catechism: Sources, History, and Theology*. Grand Rapids: Baker Academic, 2005.

————. *The Theology of the Heidelberg Catechism: A Reformation Synthesis*. Louisville, KY: Westminster John Knox, 2013.

Billings, J. Todd. "John Calvin's Soteriology: On the Multifaceted 'Sum' of the Gospel." *International Journal of Systematic Theology* 11 (2009) 428–47.

————. "John Calvin: United to God through Christ." In *Partakers of the Divine* Nature, edited by Michael J. Christensen and Jeffery A. Wittung, 200–218. Madison, NJ: Fairleigh Dickinson University Press, 2007.

————. *Union with Christ: Reframing Theology and Ministry for the Church*. Grand Rapids: Baker, 2011.

Boekestein, William. *The Quest for Comfort: The Story of the Heidelberg Catechism*. Grand Rapids: Reformation Heritage, 2011.

Boston, Thomas. *The Complete Works of the Late Rev. Thomas Boston, Ettrick*. Collected Papers. Edited by Rev. Samuel M'Millan. 12 vols. London: William Tegg and Co., 1854.

Bruggink, Donald J. *Guilt, Grace, and Gratitude: A Commentary on the Heidelberg Catechism Commemorating Its 400th Anniversary*. New York: Half Moon, 1969.

Buchanan, James. *The Doctrine of Justification: An Outline of Its History in the Church and of Its Exposition from Scripture*. London: Banner of Truth, 1962.

Burge, Gary M. *Letters of John: NIV Application Commentary*. Grand Rapids: Zondervan, 1996.

Burgess, Anthony. *Spiritual Refining: Or a Treatise of Grace and Assurance*, 1652. Reprint, Ames, Iowa: International Outreach, 1990.

Burke, Trevor J. *Adopted into God's Family: Exploring a Pauline Metaphor*. Downers Grove: InterVarsity, 2006.

————. *The Message of Sonship: At Home in God's Household*. Downers Grove: InterVarsity, 2011.

Calvin, John. *Commentary on Galatians and Ephesians*. Grand Rapids: Baker, 1979.

————. *Institutes of the Christian Religion*. Translated by Ford Lewis Battles, edited by John T. McNeill. 2 vols. Louisville, KY: Westminster John Knox, 2006.

Campbell, Constantine R. *Paul and Union with Christ: An Exegetical and Theological Study*. Grand Rapids: Zondervan, 2012.

Carson, D. A. "Johannine Perspectives on the Doctrine of Assurance." *Explorations* 10 (1996) 59–97.

————. "Reflections on Christian Assurance." *Westminster Theological Journal* 54.1 (1992) 1–29.

Chang, Paul. "John Calvin on the Doctrine of Assurance." ThM thesis, Westminster Theological Seminary, 1992.

Clark, R. Scott. *Recovering the Reformed Confession: Our Theology, Piety, and Practice.* Phillipsburg, NJ: P & R, 2008.

Cranfield, C. E. B. *A Critical and Exegetical Commentary on the Epistle to the Romans.* London: T. & T. Clark, 2004.

Cunningham, William. *The Reformers and the Theology of the Reformation.* London: Banner of Truth, 1967.

Danker, Frederick William, ed. *A Greek-English Lexicon of the New Testament and Other Early Christian Literature.* 3rd ed. Chicago: University of Chicago Press, 2000.

DeYoung, Kevin L. *The Good News We Almost Forgot: Rediscovering the Gospel in a 16th Century Catechism.* Chicago: Moody, 2010.

Dickson, David. *Truth's Victory over Error: A Commentary on the Westminster Confession of Faith.* Carlisle, PA: Banner of Truth, 2007.

Dunn, James D. G. *Romans 1–8.* Word Biblical Commentary 38A. Dallas: Word, 2002.

Eaton, Michael A. *No Condemnation: A Theology of Assurance of Salvation.* 2nd ed. Downers Grove: InterVarsity, 2011.

Ecumenical Creeds and Reformed Confessions. Christian Reformed Church. Grand Rapids: Faith Alive Christian Resources, 1988.

Edwards, James R. *Romans,* New International Biblical Commentary. Peabody: Hendrickson, 1992.

Edwards, Jonathan. *The Works of Jonathan Edwards, A.M.: With an Essay on His Genius and Writings.* Vol. 2, edited by Edward Hickman. London: W. Ball, 1839.

Evans, William B. *Imputation and Impartation: Union with Christ in American Reformed Theology.* Milton Keynes, UK: Paternoster, 2008.

Fee, Gordon D. *God's Empowering Presence: The Holy Spirit in the Letters of Paul.* Peabody, MA: Hendrickson, 1994.

Ferguson, Sinclair B. *Children of the Living God.* Carlisle, PA: Banner of Truth, 2011.

———. *The Holy Spirit: Contours of Christian Theology.* Downers Grove: InterVarsity, 1996.

———. "The Teaching of the Confession." In *The Westminster Confession in the Church Today: Papers Prepared for the Church of Scotland Panel on Doctrine,* edited by Alasdair I. C. Heron, 28–39. Edinburgh: St. Andrew, 1982.

———. *The Whole Christ: Legalism, Antinomianism, and Gospel Assurance—Why the Marrow Controversy Still Matters.* Wheaton: Crossway, 2016.

Fesko, John V. *Beyond Calvin: Union with Christ and Justification in Early Modern Reformed Theology (1517–1700).* Göttingen: Vandenhoeck & Ruprecht, 2012.

———. *The Covenant of Redemption: Origins, Development, and Reception.* Gottingen: Vandenhoeck & Ruprecht, 2016.

Fitzmyer, Joseph. *Romans: A New Translation with Introduction and Commentary.* Vol. 33. New Haven, CT: Yale University Press. 2008.

Fitzpatrick, Elyse M. *Found in Him: The Joy of the Incarnation and Our Union with Christ.* Wheaton: Crossway, 2013

Frame, John. *Systematic Theology: An Introduction to Christian Belief.* Phillipsburg, NJ: P & R, 2013.

Gaffin, Richard B., Jr. *The Centrality of the Resurrection: A Study in Paul's Soteriology.* Grand Rapids: Baker Biblical Monograph, 1987.

————. *By Faith, Not by Sight: Paul and the Order of Salvation*. 2nd ed. Phillipsburg, NJ: P & R, 2016.

————. "The Holy Spirit." *Westminster Theological Journal* 43.1 (1980) 58–78.

————. "Justification and Union with Christ." In *A Theological Guide to Calvin's Institutes: Essays and Analysis*, edited by David W. Hall and Peter A. Lillback, 248–69. Phillipsburg, NJ: P & R, 2008.

————. "Redemption and Resurrection: An Exercise in Biblical-Systematic Theology." *Themelios* 27.2 (2002) 16–31.

————. *Resurrection and Redemption: A Study in Paul's Soteriology*. Phillipsburg, NJ: P & R, 1987.

————. "Union with Christ: Some Biblical and Theological Reflections." In *Always Reforming: Explorations in Systematic Theology*, edited by A. T. B. McGowan, 271–88. Downers Grove: InterVarsity, 2006.

Garcia, Mark. *Life in Christ: Union with Christ and Twofold Grace in Calvin's Theology*. Milton Keynes, UK: Paternoster, 2008.

Garner, David B. *Sons in the Son: The Riches and Reach of Adoption in Christ*. Phillipsburg, NJ: P & R, 2016.

Gerstner, John H., et al. *A Guide to the Westminster Confession of Faith: Commentary*. Signal Mountain, TN: Summertown, 1992.

Gilbert, Greg. *Assured: Discover Grace, Let Go of Guilt, and Rest in Your Salvation*. Grand Rapids: Baker, 2019.

Girardeau, John L. *Discussions of Theological Questions*. Richmond, VA: Presbyterian Committee of Publication, 1905.

Griffith, Howard "'The First Title of the Spirit': Adoption in Calvin's Soteriology." *Evangelical Quarterly* 73.2 (2001) 135–53.

Grudem, Wayne. *Systematic Theology*. Grand Rapids: Zondervan, 2000.

Gundersen, David A. "Adoption, Assurance, and the Internal Testimony of the Holy Spirit." *Journal of Family Ministry* 2.1 (2011) 18–35.

Gundry, Robert H. "Grace, Works, and Staying Saved in Paul." *Biblica* 66.1 (1985) 1–38.

Guthrie, George H. *The Structure of Hebrews: A Text-Linguistic Analysis*. Grand Rapids: Baker, 1998.

Hagner, Donald A. *Matthew 1–13*. Word Biblical Commentary 33A. Dallas: Word, 2002.

Harrison, Everett F. "Romans." In *Romans through Galatians*, edited by F. E. Gaebelein, 10:1–172. Grand Rapids: Zondervan, 1976.

Hart, John F. "Paul as Weak in Faith in Romans 7:7–25." *Bibliotheca Sacra* 170 (2013) 317–43.

Hartman, Lars. "Baptize 'Into the Name of Jesus' and Early Christology." *Studia Theologica* 28 (1974) 21–48.

————. "Into the Name of Jesus." *New Testament Studies* vol. 20 (1974) 432–40.

Hazlett, Ian. "Reformed Theology in Confessions and Catechisms to c.1620." In *The History of Scottish Theology*, edited by David Fergusson and Mark W. Elliott, 1:189–209. Oxford: Oxford University Press, 2019.

Heim, Erin M. *Adoption in Galatians and Romans: Contemporary Metaphor Theories and the Pauline Huiothesia Metaphors*. Leiden: Brill, 2017.

Helm, Paul. *Calvin and the Calvinists*. Edinburgh: Banner of Truth, 1982.

Hewitt, C. M. Kempton. *Life in the Spirit: A Study in the History of Interpretation of Romans 8:12–17*. PhD diss., Durham University, 1969.

Horton, Michael S. *Covenant and Salvation: Union with Christ.* Louisville, KY: Westminster John Knox, 2007.

Hoskinson, Matthew C. *Assurance of Salvation: Implications of a New Testament Theology of Hope.* Greenville, SC: Bob Jones University Press, 2010.

Johnson, Marcus Peter. *One with Christ: An Evangelical Theology of Salvation.* Wheaton: Crossway, 2013.

Kelly, Douglas F. "Adoption: An Underdeveloped Heritage of the Westminster Standards." *Reformed Theological Review* 52 (1993) 110–20.

Kendall, R. T. *Calvin and English Calvinism to 1649.* Oxford: Oxford University Press, 1979.

Kruse, Colin G. *The Letters of John.* Pillar New Testament Commentary. Grand Rapids: Eerdmans, 2000.

———. *Paul's Letter to the Romans.* Pillar New Testament Commentary. Grand Rapids: Eerdmans, 2012.

Law, Robert. *The Tests of Life: A Study of the First Epistle of St. John.* 3rd ed. Grand Rapids: Baker, 1979. First published 1914 by Edinburgh: T. & T. Clark.

Letham, Robert. "The Relationship between Saving Faith and Assurance of Salvation." ThM thesis, Westminster Theological Seminary, 1976.

———. "Saving Faith and Assurance in Reformed Theology: Zwingli to the Synod of Dort." PhD diss., University of Aberdeen, 1979.

———. *Union with Christ: In Scripture, History, and Theology.* Philipsburg, NJ: P & R, 2011.

———. *The Westminster Assembly: Reading Its Theology in Historical Context.* Phillipsburg, NJ: P & R, 2009.

Levin, Yigal. "Jesus, 'Son of God' and 'Son of David': the 'Adoption' of Jesus into the Davidic Line." *Journal for the Study of the New Testament* 28.4 (2006) 415–42.

Lewis, Robert Brian. *Paul's "Spirit of Adoption" in Its Roman Imperial Context.* London: T. & T. Clark, 2016.

Lloyd-Jones, Martyn. *The Assurance of Our Salvation (Studies in John 17): Exploring the Depth of Jesus' Prayer for His Own.* Wheaton: Crossway, 2000.

Luther, Martin. "Lectures on Genesis 21–25." *Luther's Works,* edited by Jaroslav Pelikan, vol. 4. St. Louis: Concordia, 1958.

———. "Lectures on Genesis 38–44." *Luther's Works,* edited by Jaroslav Pelikan, vol. 7. St. Louis: Concordia, 1958.

———. *Martin Luther's Basic Theological Writings,* edited by Timothy F. Lull. Minneapolis: Fortress, 1989.

Macaskill, Grant. *Union with Christ in the NT.* Oxford: Oxford University Press, 2013.

Master, Jonathan. *A Question of Consensus: The Doctrine of Assurance after the Westminster Confession.* Minneapolis: Fortress, 2015.

Masters, Peter. *Faith, Doubts, Trials, and Assurance.* Oberlin, OH: Wakeman, 2006.

McCant, Jerry. "A Wesleyan Interpretation of Romans 5–8." *Wesleyan Theological Journal* 16.1 (1981) 68–84.

Moo, Douglas J. *The Epistle to the Romans.* New International Commentary on the New Testament. Grand Rapids: Eerdmans, 1996.

———. *Romans.* NIV Application Commentary. Grand Rapids: Zondervan, 2000.

Morris, Leon. *The Epistle to the Romans.* Grand Rapids: Eerdmans, 1988.

Mounce, Robert H. *Romans: An Exegetical and Theological Exposition of Holy Scripture,* New American Commentary. Nashville: Broadman & Holman, 1995.

Muller, Richard. *The Unaccommodated Calvin*. New York: Oxford University Press, 2000.

Murray, John. *Collected Writings of John Murray*. Vol. 2. Carlisle, PA: Banner of Truth, 1977.

———. *The Epistle to the Romans*. Vol. 1. New International Commentary on the New Testament. Grand Rapids: Eerdmans, 1959.

———. *Redemption Accomplished and Applied*. Grand Rapids: Eerdmans, 1955.

Noll, Mark A. "John Wesley and the Doctrine of Assurance." *Bibliotheca Sacra* 132.526 (1975) 161–77.

Owen, John. *The Works of John Owen*. Vol. 1. Edited by W. H. Goold. London: Banner of Truth, 1987.

Packer, J. I. "Assurance." In *New Bible Dictionary*, edited by I. Howard Marshall et al., 95–96. 3rd ed. Downers Grove: InterVarsity, 1996.

———. *Concise Theology: A Guide to Historic Christian Beliefs*. Wheaton: Tyndale, 1993.

———. *Knowing God*. Downers Grove: InterVarsity, 1993.

Peppard, Michael. *The Son of God in the Roman World: Divine Sonship in Its Social and Political Context*. New York: Oxford University Press, 2011.

Perkins, William. *A Golden Chain: The Description of Theology*. 1597. Reprint, Waitakere, New Zealand: Titus, 2014.

———. *The Works of That Famous and Worthy Minister of Christ in the Universitie of Cambridge, Mr. William Perkins*. Vols. 1–2. London: John Legatt, 1626, 1631.

Peterson, Robert A. *Adopted by God: From Wayward Sinners to Cherished Children*. Phillipsburg, NJ: P & R, 2001.

———. *The Assurance of Salvation: Biblical Hope for Our Struggles*. Grand Rapids: Zondervan, 2019.

———. "Christian Assurance: Its Possibility and Foundations." *Presbyterion* 18.1 (1992) 10–24.

———. *Our Secure Salvation: Perseverance and Apostasy*. Phillipsburg, NJ: P & R, 2009.

———. *Salvation Applied by the Spirit: Union with Christ*. Wheaton: Crossway, 2015.

Pfürtner, Stephen. *Luther and Aquinas on Salvation*. Translated by Edward Quinn. New York: Sheed & Ward, 1964.

Phillips, Richard D. "Assured in Christ." In *Assured by God: Living in the Fullness of God's Grace*, edited by Burk Parsons, 69–86. Phillipsburg, NJ: P & R, 2006.

Pink, Arthur W. *Gleanings in Exodus*. Lafayette, IN: Sovereign Grace, 2002.

Ridderbos, Herman. *Paul: An Outline of His Theology*, translated by J. R. de Witt. Grand Rapids: Eerdmans, 1975.

Rivera, Eric. *Christ Is Yours: The Assurance of Salvation in the Puritan Theology of William Gouge*. Bellingham, WA: Lexham, 2019.

Rockwell, Stephen. "Assurance as the Interpretive Key to Understanding the Message of 1 John." *Reformed Theological Review* 69.1 (2010) 17–33.

Rogers, John. *The Doctrine of Faith: Wherein Are Practically Handled Twelve Principall Points, Which Explaine the Nature and Vse of It*. London: N. Newbery and H. Overton, 1629.

Schaff, Philip. *The Creeds of Christendom*. 3 vols. New York: Harper and Brothers, 1919.

Schreiner, Thomas, and Ardel Caneday. *The Race Set Before Us: A Biblical Theology of Perseverance and Assurance*. Downers Grove: InterVarsity, 2001.

Scott, James M. *Adoption as Sons of God: An Exegetical Investigation into the Background of YIOTHESIA in the Pauline Corpus.* Wissenschaftliche Untersuchungen zum Neuen Testament 2/48. Tübingen: J. C. B. Mohr (Paul Siebeck), 1992.

Sibbes, Richard. *The Works of Richard Sibbes, D.D.* Vol. 2. Edited by Alexander Balloch Grosart. Edinburgh: J. Nichol, 1862.

Smedes, Lewis B. *Union with Christ: A Biblical View of the New Life in Jesus Christ.* Grand Rapids: Eerdmans, 2009.

Snoddy, Richard. *The Soteriology of James Ussher: The Act and Object of Saving Faith.* Oxford: Oxford University Press, 2014.

Sproul, R. C. *Truths We Confess: A Layman's Guide to the Westminster Confession of Faith.* Vol. 2. Phillipsburg, NJ: P & R, 2007.

Stanglin, Keith D. *Arminius on the Assurance of Salvation: The Context, Roots, and Shape of the Leiden Debate, 1603–1609.* Leiden: Brill, 2007.

Stoeffler, F. Ernest. "The Wesleyan Concept of Religious Certainty—Its Pre-history and Significance." *London Quarterly and Holborn Review*, 6.33 (1964) 128–39.

Tipton, Lane G. "Union with Christ and Justification." In *Justified in Christ: God's Plan for Us in Justification*, edited by K. Scott Oliphint, 23–49. Fearn, UK: Mentor, 2007.

Torrance, James B. "Strengths and Weaknesses of the Westminster Theology." In *The Westminster Confession in the Church Today: Papers Prepared for the Church of Scotland Panel on Doctrine*, edited by Alasdair I. C. Heron, 40–54. Edinburgh: St. Andrew, 1982.

Trueman, Carl R. *The Creedal Imperative.* Wheaton: Crossway, 2012.

Trumper, Tim J. R. "From Slaves to Sons." *Foundations* 55 (2006) 17–19.

———. "The Theological History of Adoption I: An account." *Scottish Bulletin of Evangelical Theology* 20.1 (2002) 4–28.

———. "The Theological History of Adoption II: A Rationale." *Scottish Bulletin of Evangelical Theology* 20.2 (2002) 177–202.

———. *When History Teaches Us Nothing: The Recent Reformed Sonship Debate in Context.* Eugene, OR: Wipf & Stock, 2008.

Venema, Cornelis. *Accepted and Renewed in Christ: The "Twofold Grace of God" and the Interpretation of Calvin's Theology.* Göttingen: Vandenhoeck & Ruprecht, 2007.

———. "Calvin's Understanding of the 'Twofold Grace of God' and Contemporary Ecumenical Discussion of the Gospel." *Mid-America Journal of Theology* 18 (2007) 67–105.

———. "Union with Christ, the "Twofold Grace of God," and the Order of Salvation in Calvin's Theology." In *Calvin for Today*, edited by Joel R. Beeke, 91–114. Grand Rapids: Reformation Heritage, 2009.

Volf, Judith M. Gundry. *Paul and Perseverance: Staying In and Falling Away.* Louisville, KY: Westminster, 1991.

Vos, Geerhardus. *Biblical Theology: Old and New Testaments.* Grand Rapids: Eerdmans, 1948.

———. "The Doctrine of the Covenant in Reformed Theology." In *Redemptive History and Biblical Interpretation: The Shorter Writings of Geerhardus Vos*, edited by Richard B. Gaffin Jr., 234–67. Phillipsburg, NJ: P & R, 1980.

Wallace, Daniel B. *Greek Grammar beyond the Basics: An Exegetical Syntax of the New Testament.* Grand Rapids: Zondervan, 1996.

———. "The Witness of the Spirit in Romans 8:16: Interpretation and Implications." https://bible.org/seriespage/2-witness-spirit-romans-816-interpretation-and-implications.

Webb, Robert Alexander. *The Reformed Doctrine of Adoption*. Harrisonburg, VA: Sprinkle, 2012.

Weir, David A. *The Origins of the Federal Theology in Sixteenth-Century Reformation Thought*. New York: Oxford University Press, 1990.

Wesley, John. *Wesley's Standard Sermons*. Edited by Edward H. Sugden. 3rd ed., 2 vols. London: Epworth, 1951.

———. *The Works of John Wesley*. 14 vols. Grand Rapids: Zondervan, 1872.

Westhead, Nigel. "Adoption in the Thought of John Calvin." *Scottish Bulletin of Evangelical Theology* 13.2 (1995) 102–15.

The Westminster Confession of Faith. 3rd ed. Lawrenceville, GA: Committee for Christian Education and Publications, 1990.

Whitney, Donald S. *How Can I be Sure I'm a Christian? The Satisfying Certainty of Eternal Life*. Colorado Springs: NavPress, 2019.

Whyte, Alexander. *An Exposition on the Shorter Catechism: Includes the Westminster Confession and the Larger Catechism*. Fearn, UK: Christian Focus, 2004.

Williamson, G. I. *The Heidelberg Catechism: A Study Guide*. Phillipsburg, NJ: P & R, 1993.

———. *The Westminster Confession of Faith for Study Classes*. Phillipsburg, NJ: P & R, 2004.

Zachman, Randall C. *The Assurance of Faith: Conscience in the Theology of Martin Luther and John Calvin*. Minneapolis: Augsburg Fortress, 1993.

Index of Names and Subjects

Index of Scripture

www.ingramcontent.com/pod-product-compliance
Lightning Source LLC
Chambersburg PA
CBHW060340100426
42812CB00003B/1066